TURN YOUR TOWN AROUND

How to Make It a Great Destination Community

GEE WILLIAMS

MAYOR, TOWN OF BERLIN, MARYLAND (2008-2020)

TURN YOUR TOWN AROUND

How to Make It a Great Destination Community

Secant Publishing, LLC
P.O. Box 4059
Salisbury, MD 21803

www.secantpublishing.com

ISBN: 979-8-9851489-5-4 (hardcover)
ISBN: 979-8-9851489-6-1 (paperback)

Library of Congress Control Number: 2022919807

CONTENTS

PREFACE

My purpose in writing this book is to help you find ways to turn your town into a joyful and prosperous place for you to live and for others to visit. Every town should strive to be known as a vibrant destination community. The time has come for towns to be recognized as special places possessed of distinct opportunities. They are not so big as to overwhelm; but they are often big enough and established enough to have rich and rewarding histories, cultures, economies, and built environments.

Over the past century, America enjoyed a sustained period of growth in jobs and economic opportunity in urban as well as suburban areas.

But economic growth, a widely sought-after measure of success, can also result in reduced quality of life and undesired side effects. These can include increased commuter traffic, a faster pace in everyday life, and a certain standardization of the "big boxes" and national chain outlets where we shop and eat. There can also be a loss of quality time to enjoy with family, neighbors, and others in our community.

This is where towns have a chance to shine. Many smaller communities have not only preserved, but even enhanced, attractive aspects of living that can be lost in highly urban areas. Some towns are charting a way towards economic and cultural revival without losing the lifestyle characteristics that citizens in metropolitan areas crave and want to enjoy.

I have a lifetime of experience in serving smaller communities that are successful in attracting visitors and guests while not losing their unique character or charm. I was a local newspaper editor and publisher for thirty years, managing publications in communities along the East Coast from Delaware to South Carolina. I also have many years of experience in marketing and public relations. It was my privilege to serve as mayor of the Town of Berlin, Maryland, for twelve years (2008—2020).

During my tenure as mayor, Berlin's downtown district became home to over fifty thriving businesses, doubling the number that previously existed. While mayor, our community received thirty unsolicited state and national awards, including being voted *"America's Coolest Small Town"* in an online contest. While my hometown of Berlin has developed a tradition of respecting and preserving historical buildings and remembering our history, I also think our community is pretty progressive for a small town. This is particularly true in matters such as environmental stewardship, racial tolerance and diversity, and economic opportunity. It is with this background in mind that I have written this book. My purpose is to inspire and help you overcome any sense of your community's complacency or acceptance of stagnation, and put your town on course for economic and cultural renewal.

First, I wish to thank Betsy, my kind and caring wife, who has provided me with constant support and encouragement throughout this journey. I am also grateful for the advice, assistance, and body of experience that was shared with me by many colleagues throughout my career, including past and current members of the Berlin mayor's office and Town Council. I also thank the many citizens who have made so much effort and contributed so many ideas towards making life better in our community for both residents and guests. In the pages that follow, I hope you will find encouragement to start transforming your community into a thriving place to live, enjoy, and share.

Now, let's take a look at your town's current status quo. Have you ever had these thoughts?

"Nothing ever really changes in our town."

"Our town survives, but never thrives."

"Somehow our town's beauty and appeal has faded with time."

"When I shop, I would prefer to have a variety of choices in our downtown."

"Would anyone recommend our town to newcomers or visitors?"

"Why do we keep doing the same old things, but expect different results?"

If you have had these or similar thoughts, then this book finds you in the right place.

In the chapters that follow I invite you to thoughtfully consider a rewarding journey of economic and cultural renewal for your town. It matters not whether you are a lifelong resident of your community, or a relative newcomer. The number of years you have been living in your town does not determine your potential influence. What makes all the difference is your ability and willingness to see and act on the possibilities for positive change that will result in long-term enjoyment and satisfaction.

In this book you will see how to chart a course of rediscovery and renewal for fellow citizens and your community's future guests. You will have the opportunity to discover how your town can flourish. You will also find new ways to share your town and build a stronger foundation for your community's success.

You will discover your community's potential for cultural and artistic appeal and learn how you can make your visitors feel welcomed, rather than looked upon as strangers. This book will also discuss the issue of proximity—how you can capitalize on your town's nearness in space or relationship to more populated areas.

It is my expectation that this book will take you on a journey of collaboration and inspire you to create special events and other enhancements to improve the quality of everyday life in your town. You can believe in your future and your town's future. It is a future that can be greatly influenced by what you believe—and what you do.

Your efforts can attract appreciative guests and be an ongoing source of enjoyment and pride for your fellow citizens. Always with an eye towards improving, your town can achieve a stronger local economy by transforming into a successful destination community. From my decades of hands-on experience with these endeavors, I believe you too can adopt the attitudes and strategies that follow. You and your fellow citizens can begin to set a course for a better future that will *"Turn Your Town Around"* for the enjoyment and economic benefit of current and future generations in your community.

CHAPTER ONE

Rediscovering Your Town's Potential for Renewal

In these times of uncertainty and invasive technology, more of us need and crave real-life interpersonal contacts and experiences. This is true whether we live in cities, towns, or rural areas. Welcoming communities understand this heartfelt need for human relationship, and accordingly, do not think of themselves as isolated fortresses. Instead, they are shining examples of what life can be when all aspects of our existence center on quality over quantity.

It's a great time to take a new look at your town. Ironically, much of its potential may be hidden in plain sight, and a new point of view can lead to a rediscovery of assets that may have been long forgotten or simply taken for granted. A new perspective should include a variety of community aspects including architectural themes, landmarks, underutilized buildings, and natural assets. The process of rediscovering your town's potential for renewal begins with defining its unique local flavor, potential for economic revival, and the enhancement or creation of local cultural assets and events. These are things you can develop with pride and enjoyment for not only local citizens, but also for potential visitors who will make your town a successful and enjoyable destination community.

First Connect and Rediscover

There is every reason to believe that after experiencing a Covid-imposed era of isolation and remote working, most people are ready for much more socialization and happier times. This will include more informal contact with people at large, not just those individuals who are already friends or acquaintances After an unprecedented era of forced or limited isolation, free and natural communications with others will be more important than ever. People are happy to see one another again without the constraints of masks and distancing, testing and quarantining. For towns and communities seeking revitalization, these are the perfect circumstances to create a brew of economic and cultural renewal.

Reinvesting Begins with Believers

The investment of time, money, and effort in your community shares the same characteristics as any other successful venture. First and foremost, you must believe in yourself and your town. This may seem obvious. But the need for *belief* is often underappreciated as a precondition for success. The initial investment you and like-minded citizens must make is to genuinely believe in your community. A believer is a person who believes something is desirable, effective, and beneficial, and that it can be achieved.

Critical to your community's success is connecting people who believe it can become an appealing and inviting place to be shared with residents and guests. The success of your community may grow over time or may happen more quickly than you expect. It is important to remember that, regardless of any disbelievers and naysayers, a collaborative and coordinated effort by like-minded citizens will succeed.

Here are examples of some questions you can discuss with your town's citizens.

- Are we living in a community that once was proud of its origins and history, but whose spirit and pride has faded with time?
- Are there physical and cultural attributes in our town that can be rediscovered or revitalized?
- What positive activities and opportunities can we add to our town's calendar?
- Can we think about and suggest ways to make our town more welcoming?

These are conversations you can undertake immediately, not just at some point in the future. You can also initiate a fresh look at your town. You can start on a small scale with one-on-one talks. In a relatively short time, you can find others who believe your town has much quality-of-life potential. Start by encouraging them to meet in small groups. These small groups get together in a variety of informal ways—at a local coffee shop, restaurant or bar, at one person's home, a workplace after hours, or even by computer via the Zoom app.

Some of the common attributes you should look for about believers in your town include people who are:

- Not inherently fearful or suspicious of people they do not know.

o Proud of their community and willing to share it.

o Welcoming and helpful when they meet visitors.

o Not easily discouraged or prone to throw in the towel when things go wrong or do not meet their expectations.

o Willing to invest their time and resources in improving their community.

Your small-group discussions should center around ways your town can transform from a place of relative isolation to an inviting and enjoyable destination. Look around and find physical and cultural attributes that can be rediscovered or revitalized. Look honestly at how visitors—your town's guests—are treated. Are they welcomed, or looked upon as outsiders and strangers? Discuss some ways you can make your town more welcoming—not sometime in the future, but now!

In Berlin, our businesses and residents began to understand that each visitor could become a regular guest and would experience more enjoyment by returning more than one time a year. By offering the same openness and friendliness that local residents had always received, the visitors soon came to see our downtown as a home away from home. This would become true not only for people who came from other smaller cities and towns but was especially evident among urban and suburban visitors who were welcomed as guests, not outsiders.

A Journey of Rebirth Begins

My hometown's journey of rebirth began in the 1970s. The Berlin mayor and council, at the urging of a handful of citizens who were history buffs, began hosting informal public meetings to discuss ideas on how to revitalize—not modernize—our town. After several of these meetings, and following a particularly long discussion back and forth, an elderly lady who resided in Berlin stood up and asked to be recognized. This lady simply said: "I've been attending these meetings and it seems to me we have only one decision to make. And that is—are we going to change or is our town going to die?" The crowded room of Berlin citizens immediately burst into loud applause and cheers. So much pent-up frustration that so many citizens had endured individually for years was spontaneously released. This was a pivotal moment for our town. Suddenly, a fresh look at our town could be not only discussed but encouraged. Certainly, the town's naysayers didn't disappear, not by a longshot, but they never regained the stranglehold on our community that they had for decades before.

Think about your community and ask yourself:

o Are you allowing the naysayers and people who just don't believe in the future of your town to undermine new initiatives and ideas?

o Is talk or consideration of any meaningful change in your town 'dead on arrival'?

o Are you resolved to overcome the skepticism and ridicule that inevitably will come your way?

o Are you committed to responding to such criticism with patience and class?

Certainly, you can expect criticism on social media, and in smaller communities you will likely also be confronted by naysayers face-to-face. For your town to succeed in transforming into an attractive destination, you must be resolved and committed to overcoming the skepticism and ridicule of your community's critics, no matter how loud they may be. People who are content with the status quo many times are easily threatened by anything that brings new opportunities. And let's be clear—that usually means they are threatened by any change to your town. Members of your community who want to keep things the same are often the most fearful of change. Generally speaking, they are fearful because they live in the past—not the distant past, but their own personal past.

Regardless of how small the number of believers you begin with, it's important that you begin. So, let's talk about your first step, building believers in your town. Please know that in the beginning not everyone, or even a majority of citizens, will believe the future can be a better place for your town. You only need enough people to get discussions started about some recognizable, tangible differences that can begin with incremental change.

By continuing your efforts with sometimes small, but repeated successes, you will build a foundation for change in your community. Inevitably your efforts, joined by others, will reach a point of critical mass, or what is described in this book as a game changer. Once discovered, this critical mass develops into momentum for even further and greater impactful change. So, how will you begin your town's renaissance?

Rediscovering Your Community's Roots

A few years ago, I was attending a local historical event and the photographer Edwin Remsberg said: "Our roots make our branches possible." That has stuck with me. I believe that for most people, our sense of place is very important to our human experience. By rediscovering your community's roots, you too can make your town unique by reclaiming its past. And by a logical process of reclaiming, redefining, and marketing your town's past, you have an opportunity to redefine not only its future but yours. Just like a tree, your community's roots make your town's branches of hospitality and economic revival possible.

Take a new look at your town's history and share the best of it. Decide what to share and promote—and yes, what to downplay or forget. Discuss what has been forgotten, or taken for granted, that can be reclaimed and revitalized. How can you make your community's past a legacy that is meaningful and beneficial today and in the future?

The Beginnings of Berlin

My hometown of Berlin started in the 1790s as a traditional colonial plantation, called Burley, which was part of an English land grant dating back to 1677. Early in the plantation's development, a tavern and overnight accommodation named the Burley Inn was constructed nearby. It was located near the crossroads of the Philadelphia Post Road (now Main Street) and Sinepuxent Road (now Bay Street). The tavern soon became a popular place to eat, drink, and sleep for visitors to the plantation. The town was first known as

"Stevenson's Crossroads," but soon became better known as the location of the Burley Inn. As a result of the strong southern accent that once dominated our region, the Burley Inn over several decades became pronounced "BURL-un". That evolved into "Berlin," which became the official name of the town when it was incorporated after the Civil War in 1868.

Sharing the Best

First, share the best—forget the rest! Decide what to share and yes, what to downplay or forget. As you start mixing your town's past with the opportunities of today, you are creating wonderful new experiences for both residents and visitors. Let's consider the economic and cultural advantages of welcoming more guests to your community. They include but are not limited to:

- The return of your town's guests throughout the year and during the holiday season to engage in gift shopping.
- The attraction of visitors who appreciate your community's values.
- Increased income for local businesses and nonprofits.
- A boost to your community's pride and reputation.
- More positive opportunities for locals to enjoy your town.
- The creation of new businesses and jobs spawned by growing hospitality.

A Prescription for Success

Born and raised in Berlin, J.E. Parker was a career pharmacist until his retirement. He not only witnessed the town's transformation firsthand, he also actively led and supported the transition of downtown into a welcoming and economically vibrant place. Immediately after college and the completion of his pharmaceutical training, Parker started working at Farlow's Pharmacy on Main Street in 1974. He also bought the building that housed the pharmacy, which John H. Farlow opened in 1910.

Shortly after purchasing the property, Parker became aware of a new state economic development program that  would help to finance commercial revitalization. He applied for and received a grant. The resulting upgrades to the pharmacy building were the earliest in Berlin's revitalization, a transformation that continues throughout downtown to this day. Parker continued to improve and adapt the pharmacy until 1996,

J.E. Parker

when he sold the business, but he continues to own the downtown property. The corner of the building is located adjacent to the convergence of three streets—Main Street, Bay Street, and William Street—which are directly across from the Hotel Atlantic.

"It is important to stick with renovation and not resort to demolition," Parker said. He noted that the corner building is very well constructed and continues to benefit from an expansion in the 1950s by Walt Savage, the owner at that time. Parker said the look of the exterior also benefited from a faux Victorian-style front that was added when downtown Main Street was the set for two major movies in the 1990s.

Parker also served as a member of the Berlin Town Council for ten years during the 1980s. It was during his service as a councilman that Berlin was approached by Maryland Economic Development to determine if the municipality was interested in having a study conducted to assess the town's potential for economic revitalization. The department's local representative was Ed White, and he would later encourage the redevelopment of the old Variety Store building that was renovated into the Renaissance Plaza. White also won the support of the Berlin mayor and council for a paid study that would determine if the Hotel Atlantic should be restored to its original look inside and out. The study highly recommended the hotel's restoration and this ultimately spurred the interest of a group of local investors in that project. The state also provided some low interest loans for downtown Berlin property owners to restore their buildings to their original late Victorian Era appearance. Parker closed the pharmacy and began advertising for vendors to rent booths to sell antiques on the first-floor level of the building. He was very pleased by the response as several booths were quickly rented. He also converted the second floor into rental apartments.

Parker soon was approached by Patricia Fisher, who owned an antiques shop on North Main Street. After looking over the site, Fisher leased the former pharmacy location and rented several more booths exclusively for the sale of antiques. Fisher had opened her first antique shop on Main Street almost thirty years ago, thereby creating momentum and appeal for renewing downtown shopping in Berlin. Her original store on North Main was previously the location of Berlin's Chevrolet auto dealership for many years.

The family's antique store, Town Center Antiques, was started by Patricia and Don Fisher. Patricia is the mother of Bill Outten, who is now carrying on the family's downtown antique businesses. The Fishers opened a second Main Street

Bill Outten

store when the site of Farlow's Pharmacy closed. Within the first year the neighboring retail property owned by John Howard Burbage closed. It had long been the Style Guide clothing store and was located immediately next to Fisher's antique store in the former pharmacy. So, Fisher signed another lease and expanded the antique business to include the entire space that had formerly been the clothing store. The expansion gave antique shoppers access to the store from entrances on both Main Street and Pitts Street, and became known as Town Center Antiques. The larger store accommodated up to two hundred booths rented to individuals who wanted to sell family antiques, and it became a major attraction for shoppers visiting downtown Berlin.

The Outten family has lived in this area for generations and continues to be a leader in the development of antique stores in Berlin as well as, more recently, a new gift store on Main Street. Today, Bill Outten continues to adapt to market trends and has converted the former Town Center location into Outten's Delights, which features a wide variety of gifts for the Christmas holiday season, nautically themed gifts, home goods, and women's supplies. He still is Berlin's leader in retail antique sales and operates two other downtown antique store locations: Pitts Street Treasures and the Uptown Emporium on South Main Street.

19th Century Charm - 21st Century Living

Lifelong Berlin resident Carol Rose was chair of the Berlin Historic District Commission. As of this writing she still serves on the HDC and is also a very active member of the nonprofit Taylor House Museum. She noted there are a number of factors that have contributed to the town's revitalization. "There is a feeling when you visit that you are in a tight-knit place where people care about each other. This provides a comforting feeling to not only the residents but also to our town's visitors. There is an appeal and a feeling of safety, of family, and of old times when people come to our town," Rose says.

In a conversation in 2011, Rose said, "Rediscovering our local history has been important to our town, and much of Berlin's early economic success was the result of the establishment and service provided by the railroad. What we are today is because of what was here and continued over many generations. People discover our roots when they see our downtown's architectural backdrop and when visiting the Taylor House Museum. Over the years many younger families have bought older homes in our town and re-stored them while preserving their historical style." She added, "We have been successful and must continue to bring younger families to town and encourage them to take hold of our historical torch of knowledge and pride. It is important that families from each generation continue to have an appreciation of our history."

Carol Rose

Special public events have been a major contributor in enabling visitors to discover and appreciate downtown Berlin. This includes the town's annual Peach Festival that was started and continues under the sponsorship of the Taylor House Museum. "The museum started the Peach Festival that is held each year in August and has become our major fundraiser and an attraction for the whole town," Rose said. "People can come any time of the day for the festival and also visit downtown. It brings many new and returning visitors each year, including many in the surrounding area and even some former residents who return to visit."

Rose said she believes many people are attracted and return to Berlin because downtown provides a diverse and charming business area. "There's a lot to look at and shop for. We not only have some really nice stores, but also several great restaurants. And it's very important that visitors are treated with friendliness and have a good experience in town every time," she added. "It's never too late to turn your town around, but it takes more than a couple of people. A core group is necessary, and as the saying goes, 'It takes a village' to make it happen."

Rose explained that it requires not only volunteers, but also the support and participation of town government, store owners, civic groups, and individuals to work together in a common effort.

Be aware that rediscovering your roots is not an attempt to document a historical record of your town's past, but rather an opportunity to rediscover and promote the positive aspects of your community. Consider ways your town can attract newcomers while promoting pride among citizens, both new and old. This is an opportunity to both create and promote new cultural and economic attractions. Regardless of how much criticism or indifference you may initially encounter, always keep in mind that doing something to plant new seeds for success is better than doing nothing.

If your downtown has some rundown, even derelict, old buildings and homes from an earlier era, don't destroy them, but assess their viability and if practical, renovate them in their original style. Demise and decay take decades, but the revitalization of your community's architectural heritage can be accomplished in only a few years and likely will take no more than a year for any one property. As momentum builds for the completion of these restorations, the impact of attracting more visitors grows with each passing year. At the turn of the 20th century, downtown Berlin was devastated by three major fires: 1895, 1901, and 1904. The three fires destroyed almost all of downtown's wooden buildings. After the first fire in 1895, the hotel's wooden predecessor was destroyed and replaced with the current brick and mortar Hotel Atlantic that was built that year in its late Victorian Era style.

Reviving a Historic Look

Dave Englehart, the Town of Berlin's director of planning and zoning, noted: "The key attributes in restoring and revitalizing a downtown are to recognize the need for attractiveness, keeping or restoring the historic architectural flavor, and business owners who believe and invest in the effort." Berlin is one of only three municipalities in Maryland that own and operate an electric utility. "We have a town that was willing to remove downtown utility poles and boxes that conflict with the historic look everyone has been working to revive." Utility poles were removed on Main Street and replaced with electric-powered classic Victorian-style street lamps.

"In Berlin the streetscape looks like a historic pedestrian mall, and we have a downtown anchor in the Hotel Atlantic," Englehart said. "Where there used to be unused downtown

Dave Englehart

stores or buildings, we now have a waiting list of businesses who want to occupy those spaces. Vacancies are rare and are quickly filled. Berlin has adapted and reused downtown buildings that in many other places were torn down." Englehart added, "In our town those revitalized buildings have made our downtown streetscape both stunning and appealing. We have maintained an effort by local government, businesses, and property owners to restore buildings to their original historic architecture where in many other places those old buildings were torn down."

He said, "I think we embraced our town slogan, '19th Century Charm – 21st Century Living,' and now we have it."

CHAPTER TWO

Building a Foundation
for Your Town's Success

I n the late 1970s, more citizens and property owners gradually began to believe in the future of our town. Beginning with open and candid discussions about its past, several citizens began to think about how our community could return to its earlier success. Although these citizens were not the cause of the town's stagnation, they accepted responsibility for the status quo. They recognized that over time the loss of a community's historical identity can lead to its ongoing economic and cultural demise.

As you and your community consider revitalization, have open and candid discussions and ask citizens if they are ready to take some responsibility for your town's current stuck-in-a-rut state of affairs. It's always appropriate to openly discuss your community's potential while not hiding from its past. These efforts should be shared and promoted not only through meetings but also in local news reports, print and broadcast media interviews, and of course social media. An advantage that's available today is the ability to create a website that can be used not only as a community forum, but also as a resource for the possibilities, events, and even hopes and dreams for the future. All this can be initiated by a small handful of believers in your town.

Businessman Bill Freeman was one of the earliest believers in the future of downtown Berlin. He bought the long-established Treasure Chest jewelry store from Doris Taylor in 1977. It was then located in what is still known as the old Odd Fellows building at the corner of Main Street and Jefferson Street. Freeman felt he needed a larger space to expand the business, so he bought a building in the center of Main Street that had housed Ralph Davis' 5 and Dime store for decades. Davis was retiring and was pleased to find a local buyer.

Freeman remodeled store inside and out with an historic Berlin look and the new Treasure Chest moved in and reopened on December 1, 1977. The store's sales started growing immediately and everyone was very encouraged by the return of the store's late Victorian style.

Two years later, Freeman and a good friend, Jim Barrett, who was co-owner of Berlin's Chevy-Olds auto dealership, bought an underutilized building across the street from the Treasure Chest. In the years prior to the purchase by Freeman and Barrett it had served as the Variety Store, a discount retail store. The building had been built in 1900 and one of the units upstairs had served as the offices of the *Berlin Advance* newspaper from 1904 to 1921.

Freeman and Barrett's first step was to remove the artificial exterior that had been overlaid on the original brick building. It was very similar to many other town commercial buildings that had undergone the same fate in the late 1940s and 1950s in an attempt to modernize American downtowns. It was also not long after World War II that railroad passenger service was discontinued on the line going through Berlin, as motor vehicles became much more accessible and affordable in the late 1940s and 1950s.

During the reconstruction of the former retail discount store, the new owners began re-modeling the first floor to accommodate four small businesses and convert the building's second level into very nice and tasteful apartments. But instead of being welcomed and encouraged, our town's naysayers openly ridiculed the revitalization efforts. These naysayers even gathered across the street from the renovation project to openly and vocally share their scorn.

Terri Sexton & Bill Freeman

"We took that building apart from top to bottom and returned it to its original late 19th century look," Freeman said. As the local newspaper editor at that time, it was apparent to me that there were almost no retail stores downtown and the upstairs had some rundown apartments. Most stores in downtown were used as legal or insurance offices and many provided storage for Ocean City businesses all year round. The restoration of the Renaissance Plaza was completed in 1982 and it won the Maryland Historical Trust's *Preservation Project Award* in 1984.

Freeman explained their approach to the restoration. "We wanted to turn the town around, so we started by making the downstairs area into four separate retail stores." Upstairs was reconstructed into three apartments. "We didn't think the units without outdoor areas were good for children, so we made each a one-bedroom apartment. Before we renovated the building the upstairs apartments had been rented for $35, but after the costs of improving those apartments, we charged $300 per month," Freeman said. "To everyone's surprise all four units were rented almost immediately, but none to families with children." The demand for upgraded apartments in downtown Berlin was noticed immediately by other landlords and it was not long afterward many renovated their units and soon rented them at the much higher rates.

"The four stores on the first floor of the former Variety Store building were also significantly upgraded and the exterior of the entire building was restored to its original late 19th century style. In a very short time all the stores were rented at the highest rental rates in town," Freeman said. This too drew great attention and the restoration of downtown along Main Street and adjacent streets continued. Freeman and Barrett very appropriately renamed the building the Renaissance Plaza and it did indeed begin a renaissance of downtown that continues into the 21st century. After decades of disappointment, the idea that people would actually rent nice apartments and open new businesses downtown was simply inconceivable to the town's nonbelievers.

But when the restoration was completed in the early fall of 1982, those nonbelievers would for the first time find themselves socially relegated to background noise. Over time, their vocal objections to returning to Berlin's past would resurface but ultimately would fade away. Just three months after the renovation of the building, all four storefronts were rented as were all three upstairs apartments. All had been leased despite the storefronts and apartments being the highest rentals in our town. The project became Berlin's first game changer towards more widespread downtown revitalization. It caused many people to look at our community with a new and positive perspective. The name of the project, *Renaissance Plaza*, would prove to be particularly apt.

"When Jim and I first started we had taken a loan with 17.5 percent interest. We didn't take a salary and just put all the rental income back into the building and towards paying off the loan in those first years. All bills were paid from the rental income and none were out-of-pocket," Freeman said. "Shortly after we opened the Renaissance Plaza we were invited to Exmore, Virginia, to explain what we had done." They spoke at a dinner that promoted historic renovation in Exmore, which has long had the distinction of being a well-preserved historic town on Virginia's Eastern Shore.

"Since the 1970s, Berlin has become envied on the Eastern Shore and beyond," Freeman said. "The town has an Ambassadors Program and it has been a tremendous thing. It is clear people are coming to Berlin to shop, not just for sightseeing." From Bill Freeman's experience being an early part of Berlin's revitalization, he said confidently, "It's never too late to change your ways." And he said that goes for both property owners and residents of any town.

After twenty-two years of owning the Treasure Chest, Freeman sold the business to his daughter, Terri Freeman Sexton, in December 1999. Terri said, "Berlin is fortunate that Dad and Jim Barrett had the foresight to see what could happen here and not allow downtown to remain rundown." Her father added, "Terri has done an excellent job and has continued to grow the business. She has been its owner for an additional twenty-two years. I'm very proud of her."

The Renaissance Plaza renovation proved to be the spark that ignited Berlin's revitalization. Following this first act of renewal, over the next eighteen years to the end of the 20th century, most of Berlin's downtown storefronts were restored to their original late 19th century architectural exteriors. The result was a Main Street backdrop where all the buildings shared their original late Victorian Era look and appeal. Within one generation, a town that had been slowly fading away was revitalized into an economic and social catalyst that attracts visitors and adds new residents.

Rebirth of the Hotel Atlantic

This rebirth of our community did not happen overnight but did gain momentum from project to project over two decades. In downtown Berlin's revitalization the second major game changer was the complete renovation of the Hotel Atlantic on Main Street. The classic late Victorian style hotel was considered a town jewel in the early 20th century prior to the development of motor vehicles. During the early decades of the Burleigh Plantation, the Berlin community was a prized stop for salesmen traveling north and south by horse and carriage. The number of salesmen also greatly accelerated with the building of a passenger and freight railroad line through town in the mid-19th century.

When these salesmen arrived by either carriage or train at the Hotel Atlantic, they would announce their arrival by pulling out drums and loudly beating them with a variety of flourishes. These salesmen would become widely known as "drummers" wherever they traveled. This was a time when there were no telephones or radios. But with the beating of drums announcing their arrival, community awareness quickly spread by word-of-mouth, not only in Berlin, but for several miles around to nearby villages and farms.

The Hotel Atlantic became very popular and successful and was a center for the Town of Berlin commercially and culturally from 1885 to 1930. But it fell on very hard times with the onslaught of America's Great Depression—and it did not recover. During the immediate post-World War II years of the late 1940s and 1950s, Berlin's long-suffering business community was enamored with the idea of transforming the town by modernizing and covering over the original late Victorian Era style of many exterior downtown buildings. So, in the late 1940s the owners of the Hotel Atlantic felt they could do their part by literally hiding its original exterior.

For generations, the front of the hotel had a large porch and a long hitching post to tie up horses, carriages, and wagons. But in the mid-20th century, the long porch was torn down and a drab two-story brick building was constructed in its place. The primary purpose of the brick building was to hide the old rundown historic hotel. Although for decades the Hotel Atlantic had been the centerpiece of the town's economic and cultural vitality, after World War II its once impressive architectural façade was hidden from site to anyone walking or driving along the two streets it faced. The drab new retail exterior was properly maintained, but the majority of the original three-story hotel was now hidden from sight and fell into even more serious disrepair. By the mid-20th century, the Hotel Atlantic had become a major eyesore and embarrassment in the heart of downtown.

Investing in Your Community

Within a year of the completion of the Renaissance Plaza project in 1982, a group of eighteen local property owners and businesspeople started meeting for the purpose of exploring the idea of purchasing, renovating, and revitalizing the old Hotel Atlantic. The potential investors initially thought of their proposed venture as primarily a restoration project. They thought most of the renovation cost would be related to taking down the unsightly post-World War II block building that had been built to hide the original hotel's exterior. They also anticipated some additional costs to spruce up the exterior and interior of the original building.

It did not take long in the hotel's restoration for the group to realize this project on Main Street was going to be much more extensive and costly than originally anticipated. They came to understand that the investment necessary to restore the Hotel Atlantic to its original late Victorian architectural charm would be something from which they would not profit. When faced with this financial dilemma, instead of walking away they moved forward with both courage and commitment. This major revitalization project sparked renewed criticism and ridicule from town naysayers.

But because of the recent revival and charming return of the Renaissance Plaza project, plus the restoration of two other properties on Main Street—the law offices of Williams, Hammond, and Moore; and the Treasure Chest jewelry store—the Hotel Atlantic owners decided to proceed with the additional investment. The amount of that second investment was not revealed and remains known only to the original investors. They were encouraged to continue with the restoration by many townspeople, Berlin property owners, and local financial institutions. The restoration of the old hotel took years, but when finished in 1992, the results were stunning. It was the discovery of a history that had rarely been talked about and few locals were aware of.

The owners of the revitalized hotel made the necessary investments to ensure the restaurant and bar were returned to their 19th century glory in both internal and exterior architecture, furnishings, and food dining services. Soon after remodeling was completed in 1992, the hotel's bar and restaurant became a popular gathering place for not only local citizens but also visitors—people who soon became considered as guests of our town. With recognition of the town's history and pride plus the hotel's aesthetics, they named the new bar and restaurant the *Drummers Café* to appropriately recognize the many salesmen who lodged there in the early years of the 20th century. Within months of the hotel's reopening, citizens and other business owners who believed in this rebirth of the historic property reached out to local news media, both newspapers and broadcast, to expand public awareness of the pride and town's accomplishments in an earlier time. Quickly, the town's long forgotten and often ignored past became a source of pride for Berlin's citizens and businesses.

As social media developed in the early years of the 21st century, the town's Chamber of Commerce, municipal government, and just plain folks—all now filled with pride—began to aggressively promote Berlin on the internet. This effort soon created a strong online presence and generated an increased awareness of our town, first locally, then in neighboring states, later throughout North America, and ultimately in some foreign countries. Timely and updated online promotion was a key marketing strategy for not only the Hotel Atlantic, but also for businesses and government in the Town of Berlin; that continues to this day. As a result of these local investments and initiatives, Berlin was now in a position to leverage its local pride. So, how can you make this happen in your town?

Finding Community Partners

First, please know that each community partner brings something of value to the table. Certainly, monetary investments are an important component, but are much more likely with a growing momentum of community support and rising expectations. Ask yourself: Are there a handful of residents, local office holders, civic and social groups, businesses, or even service organizations in your community that are willing to invest some of their time, effort, and creativity into this effort? When you start, expect reluctance and resistance. But as you grow interest and support from these diverse groups, you will build momentum for the changes needed to make your community a better place. In any town, a fortunate few have the financial resources to make direct monetary investments. But other sources of money can be brought to the table through fundraising, and local and state grants.

In smaller towns and communities, everyone has something to offer. Among your earliest priorities are to identify which individuals, groups, and businesses can best fulfill your town's opportunities for positive change. By making well thought-out and sustained efforts to openly and vigorously self-examine your community, you will find more than one path to attract new visitors and independent businesses. In making the effort to reach out to your community's potential partners you can begin rebuilding local pride and attracting new visitors—or as we now say—guests. You can do this by identifying cultural events, festivals, local boutique shopping, and the development of dining and hospitality options that not only build on your local cuisine, but also appeal to a variety of other popular palates and tastes. By taking this approach and building your town's appeal incrementally—sometimes with small changes—you will inevitably discover and create the game changer that will ultimately turn your town into a destination community.

A place you will be proud to share.

CHAPTER THREE

Welcoming Guests:
The Key to Revitalization

So, what is the catalyst, the foundational change, that can get your town on track to overcoming stagnation and drift? The key is to transform your community into a thriving destination community. This will bring about both economic and cultural renewal, but without losing your town's identity or charm. Many smaller destination communities greatly benefit from day visits where guests come to town for a day or evening, but return to their homes, nearby cities, or resorts overnight. Visitors have an innate desire to share and experience the values and culture of your community, even though they stay for a relatively short time.

What is meant by destination community? The most common understanding is that a destination community is a town or smaller city that benefits from significant economic benefits by welcoming visitors while remaining livable and engaging for both full- and part-time residents. Some part-time residents may be seasonal or may enjoy your community for short stays throughout the year. In the Town of Berlin's experience, some guests are accommodated overnight at the revitalized historic Hotel Atlantic or one of the community's very nice bed and breakfast inns. The town also greatly benefits from people who are visiting area attractions or nearby resort areas. Some visitors who are simply passing through stop in downtown as they travel between nearby regional destinations.

Over time, the driving force for revitalization becomes a reliable influx of day guests who are attracted to the special activities and culture of your community.

The arrival of these guests will be influenced by the seasons, holidays, and special events. The more ways you encourage your community to be attractive and welcoming, the more reliably your town will benefit from the economic impact of your guests. By making your community's offerings classy and cool, you will attract guests who have the financial ability to enjoy your town, and thereby, help to preserve a high quality of life for everyone.

New Visitors Build Success

Jan Quick

"Towns go through cycles and Berlin is no different, but I think most people recognize our town wouldn't have seen its growth and renewal without attracting new visitors," Jan Quick said. She and her husband, Jim, own and operate the Holland House bed and breakfast.

"Now we have many places that have great shopping, great food, and a great place to enjoy and socialize," Quick added, "because of our slower pace of life. Most B&B visitors are looking for a place unlike Ocean City. This is not a place where you eat it and beat it. They want to experience the best of small-town living. Over the years the main draw has become shopping, eating, and special events. Two of the early events that set the town on course for more visitors were the Spring Celebration and the Fiddler's Convention. Today we have something going on in this town every month to attract visitors."

With marketing and promotion and pricing, visitors will want to enjoy the same beauty and ambience that are the pride of residents. Both your guests and local residents will share in the enjoyment and appreciation of small-town charm. This will become apparent in every aspect of your community.

Quality Over Quantity

An underlying principle to *Turn Your Town Around* is simply this. Choose quality over quantity in all things. And yes, progress and success always come with a price, but remember it will be your guests who ultimately bear most of the expense needed to create and sustain community renewal. After the upgrading and revitalization of our downtown, the cost of leases went up, but the demand for these leases far exceeded anything that had been seen in generations. In twenty years, the number of new businesses more than doubled to over fifty retail art and cultural-related shops. All of these businesses are owned locally and none are branches of regional or national chains. As of this writing, Berlin has multiple places to dine and drink in a community that is now home to just under 5,000 residents. By the way, the majority of those businesses are owned and operated by women. And I can't help but wonder what those men who hosted the early town re-vitalization meetings back in the 1970s would think of that!

Revitalization's Community Catalysts

Ivy Wells, Berlin's director of Economic and Community Development, believes from her experience that the road to a town's revitalization begins with just a few people: "Citizens who want to make a change, and local government represented by the mayor and council. It takes one person to put the idea out there and then one more person to agree, and that is how it spreads. This sets off a chain reaction that can result in real change," she said.

"You need to ask the local residents and businesses first,

Ivy Wells

how the town needs to adapt to provide the hours of operation, the types of products, and in what ways they can be stewards of the community. They also make it possible to have activities and events that both locals and visitors enjoy," Wells added. Local businesses are the frontline of making a welcoming impression on our town's guests. "By being friendly, it makes everyone feel like family," Wells explained. "It is important that people can return to their homes and say, *I stopped in this Berlin shop and they were so nice and helpful.* This is because a majority of our downtown business owners actually live here. They have a sense of pride in place and it shows."

Spreading the Word Shares Success

While providing a variety of experiences, tastes, and goods is important to long-term economic vitality, the collaboration in promoting local businesses is often an unfulfilled opportunity in many communities. It can start as simply as sharing and promoting information about other businesses in the town. Your town's visitors—guests—will not be shy asking questions about where to find goods or experiences when they visit. Each downtown business has the opportunity to be a source for referrals for each other. In my community the local businesses coordinate multiple tours every year exclusively for both Berlin and regional private enterprises and services. These tours enable local business owners and their employees to be guided through both new and long-established downtown businesses. It gives every business on Main Street and throughout the rest of downtown an opportunity to share their unique offerings with fellow business neighbors. Everyone on these tours is someone who will come in contact with many individuals and groups who shop in town during the year.

Open communication and cooperation are important components to growing businesses in your downtown. Businesses that were rare or did not previously exist can be important contributors to your town's future. Prior to the revitalization of downtown, my community had only one antique shop. But in a matter of just a few short years Berlin had three shops that sell quality antiques and has developed the reputation as a go-to place for antique shopping. By adopting an attitude of mutual support and cooperation instead of cutthroat competition, our downtown has artistic appeal to shoppers that includes art shops, galleries and painting studios, 3D sculpting, photography, printing, blown glass, handmade jewelry, wreaths, nature-based floral gifts, and even artistic re-creations of marine life. Downtown Berlin has twenty places to eat and drink, including nine that are full-service restaurants. There are also another thirty-two shops offering a variety of goods that attract both locals and visitors. Locally crafted artwork sold downtown includes paintings, handcrafted jewelry, and books. Berlin is also home to art galleries and the headquarters and studio for the Worcester County Art Council.

Another attraction for both locals and visitors is eight downtown restaurants and shops providing live music venues year-round. They are popular no matter the season of the year and are complemented by much larger outdoor stages during the town's twenty-two annual downtown events. Among these events each year are the three-day Berlin Fiddlers Convention in September and two New Year's Eve celebrations, one for kids at 6 p.m. and another at midnight for adults. This variety of businesses and attractions did not appear overnight but became possible because residents and businesses stopped fearing or ignoring newcomers and visitors, and started welcoming them. Another benefit to hosting multiple events is that they have become part of the tradition and pride residents of all ages have in their community.

Under Ivy Wells's leadership, Berlin's downtown Farmers Market has been taken to a whole new level. Held each Sunday from May through September at 8 a.m. to 1 p.m., the

Farmers Market includes numerous fresh food and art vendors plus enjoyable live music.

A Central Place of Welcoming

A first step to consider is to convert your Chamber of Commerce office into serving primarily as a welcome center. This may start out in your Chamber's existing space, but be sure to get your visitor center in front of your guests in a prominent place downtown. Create special brochures and handouts that promote the positive aspects of your downtown and community. Be sure to include a calendar of events about anything that may entice your guests to return later in the year. It is also important to provide your downtown brochures, guides, and maps in a weather-protected enclosed area that is accessible to the public every day at any time of day or night. It is also important to restock these items regularly or whenever they may get soiled or damaged.

It is very important to regularly update and promote your business community's website. This is a separate site from the official municipal website, but it can be listed by your town's online presence with something front and center that says "Click here for shopping and events" and immediately links the user to your downtown website. A change in attitude that is important for your existing businesses to adopt is that you are not competitors but are all partners in promoting your town. As business neighbors everyone can greatly benefit through cross-promotion and support.

Looking beyond your downtown, there is another effective way of partnering with and complementing other businesses in the region where historically only competitiveness is commonly assumed. Reach out to neighboring Chambers of Commerce. No one place can offer everything to everyone, but through collaboration you can expand knowledge of your downtown far beyond its borders. Your town's promotional materials can also be distributed through frequently visited places in your community. One suggestion is to put together some of your Chamber's brochures promoting businesses in your town and gather them together with rubber bands. These packets of brochures and a map of your downtown can easily be handed out when folks are visiting, and by cooperating with regional Chambers, they can also be distributed in nearby communities. This will be very helpful when regional visitors are looking for one-day road trips; they will discover that your town is both easily available and attractive. Since all Chambers create printed brochures and other materials promoting their community and events, you can reach out and ask them if they will give you some materials to display in your Chamber office and visitor center.

Helpful Hometown Ambassadors

In my hometown, the idea was suggested that a portable, manned booth be set up on Main Street to hand out packets of brochures and maps of downtown. During warm weather months, a temporary information booth—basically a modified speaker podium and umbrella—was moved into place on Main Street with a hand cart. It was staffed by volunteers who became known as Berlin Ambassadors. These volunteer ambassadors are pleased to share their town pride. They also benefit from the knowledge and detail gained by joining one or more of the Berlin Ambassador tours held each year that are guided by both new and long-established downtown businesses. When approached by our town's guests, the ambassadors make multiple suggestions that improve the experience of the visitors. This also enables them to provide directions and downtown maps with handwritten notations to assist town guests. Volunteer ambassadors continue to serve at the town's visitor center on Main Street throughout the week and during special events.

Learning to Love Locks

Berlin Commons is a relatively new outdoor setting just off Main Street between Gay Street and Jefferson Street, behind the Hotel Atlantic. Jeffrey Auxer Designs Blown Glass Gallery & Studio is immediately adjacent to the Commons. Auxer built artistic iron-railed panels that he placed on Gay Street in back of his studio. Based on ideas he has seen when traveling to other areas, the panels create permanent locations where anyone, Berlin residents or visitors, can freely attach locks. Auxer calls this set-up Berlin Love Locks. Each lock is

Jeff Auxer

marked with names, dates, initials, or family name. This enables the public to have an interactive way to put a personal piece of Berlin here that will remain for years.

"This is not something you have to pay for," Auxer said. "But it encourages people to return more than one time a year. By offering the same openness and friendliness as local residents have always received, the visitors soon came to see our downtown as a home away from home."

Serving Welcomed Guests

"It is hard to get someone who is enjoying a vacation at the beach to make their first drive to a nearby town, but by having special events and making their visit enjoyable, our visitors feel welcomed," noted Ivy Wells, Berlin's director of economic and community development. "Over the years for many beachgoers, Berlin has become their vacation shopping destination. Once they have seen our town, a trip to Berlin's downtown becomes a part of their trips to the beach," she added. "They sip and stroll their way through our town and once they come, they keep coming back."

An example of this welcoming attitude happened on our Main Street. A visitor was shopping in one of the local businesses and after looking over many items for a gift she told the owner, "I like your store, but I just don't see what I'm looking for." The shop owner asked if she could be more specific. When the out-of-town shopper (guest) explained the type of gift she sought, the store owner said, "I know where you can get exactly what you want." She then turned to her assistant and asked her to watch the store because she was going to escort the shopper to another business downtown and find her that perfect gift.

The shop owner walked a couple of blocks down the street with the visitor and introduced her to another shop owner. The short excursion was a success and the shopper found just the gift she had sought for a friend. After the purchase was completed, the store owner returned to her own shop, not expecting anything other than the satisfaction of helping someone to purchase a gift. But to her surprise in the days and weeks that followed, through social media, the visiting shopper widely shared her great experience shopping in Berlin. Over time, this resulted in many additional new shoppers from other communities. And the lady she assisted in buying a gift at another downtown store still returns to visit her shop and others in downtown each time she is in the vicinity of Berlin. This shopper was treated as a welcomed guest, not a stranger, and it made a lasting impact among our local shop owners and employees that benefits downtown businesses to this day.

CHAPTER FOUR

Turning Adversity into Advantage

During most of the 20th century, my town steadily fell into the shadow of the growth and popularity of a nearby seaside resort, Ocean City, Maryland. The number of visitors in the beach town between the Memorial Day and Labor Day holidays has risen from just several hundred in the late 1890s to more than 300,000 daily now. It was during these decades of growing popularity on the resort coast that the economic vitality and civic pride of nearby Berlin took a significant hit. Despite the ever-increasing number of visitors who traveled to Ocean City, the community of Berlin was left behind.

But in recent years, Ocean City's proximity has become an asset for our town rather than a liability. Neither Berlin residents nor business owners wanted to see the town overwhelmed by visitors. In the early years of revitalization, such a concern was barely imaginable. The challenge and opportunity would be to find a balance between the residential population of our town and the number of visitors we could graciously host. One of the common agreements among residents and businesses is that instead of losing our small-town charm, we need to find a way to support and enhance this important characteristic while also hosting more guests. Rather than emphasizing competition and increasing the number of our town's overnight accommodations, Berlin's efforts instead emphasized making it a successful destination community.

It became apparent that many of our town's visitors lived or stayed overnight in a place that was within a day's driving distance. They were nearby resort vacationers, or people who were traveling between other destinations. It also became obvious that by setting standards through pricing and behavior our town would not become overwhelmed or intimidated by our guests. Instead, over the years, many visitors have become part of our community's extended family. This means Berlin residents wake up each morning to a slow pace of life, put out the welcome mat, and tidy up. Then in late morning we begin welcoming daytime visitors to town who shop and eat in our historic downtown. After a day of shopping and dining in our downtown, by late afternoon or early evening our temporary guests either return to the coastal resort area, travel to another destination, or just return to their hometowns.

A recent example of overcoming adversity occurred during the three-year Covid pandemic era from 2020–2022. Our downtown businesses were thrown for a loop in the first months of this crisis. The summer of 2020 was the first in many years when the number of visitors dropped compared to the past. A few businesses closed, including three of the town's downtown restaurants. In less than six months after their closing, two of the three restaurants were reopened under new ownership. Both locations maintained some of the popular aspects that had been an attraction in the past, but also significantly tweaked their menu selections to make their establishments unique.

The greatest impact of the pandemic was a measurable loss in the number of out-of-town visitors who supported local businesses. In the early stages, most downtown hospitality venues added delivery services to serve their customers' homes and workplaces. While indoor dining dropped, diminishing the number of customers overall, there was a noticeable increase of people who ordered carryout meals. There was also a significant new demand for hospitality businesses to deliver food and drink to homes and businesses.

As a result, downtown restaurants adapted their menus to make them carryout-friendly. To accommodate the larger number of carryout customers, some of the eateries created safe, large, and easily accessible on-site spots for the pickup of food orders. Several restaurants set up outdoor bars on their properties. Some were weatherized with the approach of colder temperatures; one added a firepit, and one restaurant created clear plastic seasonal walls and canopies to keep out wind, rain, and snow. All of these alternatives for outdoor dining quickly became popular downtown attractions.

Most downtown restaurant owners did not have outdoor property, so they appealed to the town's elected leaders and received approval to set up outdoor café-style dining on the sidewalks in front, or along the side of their locations. The bottom line of our downtown's coping strategies is that Covid did not take our town down. But instead, through creative adaptation and support from the larger community, businesses and hospitality venues quickly rebounded to levels of activity and income that now exceed the pre-pandemic era. The community's response to this unforeseen worldwide health crisis is a very recent high-profile example of *Turning Adversity into*

Advantage. But it was the most likely response of a downtown that had long adopted an attitude and belief that challenges, large and small, and criticism to change, should be channeled into creative and positive responses.

Your Town's Potential: Ten Questions

Let's begin by thinking about your community as it currently is. Here are ten questions to ask yourself about your town:

- What you are most proud of about your community?
- Does its appearance have a dominant style? If not, are there even a few buildings with architecture or settings that reflect a look or feel that is unique to your area, from a time in the past, or that you are simply proud of?
- Is there a landmark in your town? Is there something visual, either manmade or natural, that is unique to your area?
- Are there a few buildings—commercial, public, or residential—that were once either historic or beautiful, but are now rundown, that can be renovated?
- Is your downtown a place that was beautiful and attractive in an earlier time, but now has lost its way architecturally and culturally?
- Do you have some natural assets or beautiful settings such as parks, waterfronts, or tree-lined lots that are underutilized, underpromoted, or even ignored?

- o Are there local foods and tasty desserts that are a source of enjoyment and pride that can be produced, promoted, and served to your community's guests?
- o Is there a music genre or local culture that your town could promote and share?
- o Are there some characters in your town's past (historical or even notorious) that you can promote and develop into an attraction?
- o Is there a date of founding, a past event, legend, or historical time that you can now use as the premise to create enjoyable public events or festivals?

When you take a fresh look at your town you may well discover there are parts of your town's past that you can reclaim with both pride and success. Please do not allow yourself to be intimidated. Even starting with a small group of individuals, you can soon discover where to start your town's journey of rediscovery and renewal.

Change for the better is most effective when residents and businesses get things done—together. Remember a very important economic driver in the success of current and potential future events or attractions are your guests, not just locally, but regionally and beyond. It is important to remember that while you are encouraging more visitors to come to your community, they are temporary guests.

Your town's economic and cultural renewal is inevitable when you bring residents and local businesses together with a shared vision of your community's future. To reach a shared vision means your first challenge is to encourage and support the citizens in your town to imagine a better future together. The art of imagining tomorrow does not need to be limited to the Disney corporate world. So, think of these folks as your town's creative engineers for a better future, or what the Walt Disney Company calls them —"*imagineers*".

By imagining, discussing, and supporting this approach you can develop a social and business environment where ideas are transformed into opportunities to make creative changes in your community. It is your responsibility to make sure such creativity is embraced, rather than feared. Not every new idea will develop to fruition, but those that are the best fits for your town will grow and ultimately ripen. It may be hard to imagine as you begin, but the attractions that these new creations foster will soon be thought of as an essential and permanent part of your community.

A Charming Approach

Bill Smith is remembered as one of the earliest believers in the revitalization of Berlin. An insurance agent in the 1970s and the owner of a real estate firm on Main Street, Smith worked to transform downtown into a viable place for both residents and visitors. As part of his efforts, Smith regularly visited state government offices and lobbied for Berlin during the annual state legislative session in Annapolis. It was during one of these visits that he learned Maryland was awarding annual Façade grants to restore commercial buildings in communities and also included grants to plant trees on main streets and adjoining downtown streets. Smith's persistent efforts to get grant support to start down revitalization in Berlin paid off.

His efforts resulted in a state grant to plant trees throughout downtown Berlin. Working with the town government, locations that had shade trees decades earlier were returned to that earlier look and feel with the planting of new trees. Many locations had once provided beauty to downtown, but as trees died they had not been replaced. Other downtown locations had not seen trees for several decades, but photos from the late 19th and early 20th centuries helped to identify where the new trees should be planted to bring back the charming Main Street ambience of an earlier time. This return of the natural beauty of the 19th century Berlin made an immediate favorable impression on both residents and visitors to downtown.

This was also a time in the late 1970s when the federal government was preparing to close the longtime Berlin Post Office on Main Street. The old post office had been located

Debbie & Steve Frene

in the building that is now the site of the Berlin Welcome Center. The U.S. Postal Service had wanted to close down the post office in downtown Berlin and move all local postal services to Ocean Pines, a new planned community, located about six miles east of Berlin.

"Dad believed that over the decades many people had been coming to Berlin to use the post office. He knew they would also shop and use

services in town," said Smith's daughter Debbie Smith Frene, founder of the Victorian Charm store on Main Street. "At that time some downtown Berlin business owners had begun debating the pros and cons of closing off Main Street to all vehicles in downtown. My dad strongly felt that if you cut out

Main Street parking you would eliminate many convenient parking spaces and ultimately kill downtown."

So at that time Bill Smith contacted local downtown property owners Louis and Bea Paglierani and worked out a deal to lease their lot on Broad Street, a couple hundred yards off Main Street, for the site of a new Berlin Post Office. After some public discussions and negotiating with the U.S. Postal Service, a deal was struck for the relocation of Berlin's post office. Debbie Frene commented, "Berlin's downtown had dodged a bullet that could have dealt a death blow to both commerce and community pride."

Debbie had worked for the Town of Berlin about 15 years, but when a store on the corner of Main and Commerce Street became available, she thought it would be ideal for a retail store. "When I opened the store, Victorian Charm, I began with the idea of selling things in Berlin that for decades people in our area had to purchase in Salisbury," about 21 miles west. "I started carrying things like wedding and birthday gifts and this evolved over the years to also include bath products, Yankee Candles, items made of pewter, and serving sets and a large selection of gift and holiday greeting cards. People would go through the collection and literally stand and laugh together as they read the cards."

Debbie Frene also noted that most of the entrepreneurs in downtown Berlin were women. This is a trait of downtown shopping and services that continues to this day. These shop owners included, but were not limited to, Terri Freeman Sexton, Janie King, Ellen Lang, Jan Quick, and Berlin banker Roxanne Williams.

Events of Enjoyment

"Early on these women, often joined by their husbands, would hang out for dinner at King's Pub, on Broad Street in downtown," Frene explained. "During these dinners we agreed that Berlin should have an event that would draw many people to our town. So, among ourselves we agreed that we should start with a Spring Celebration as the colder, slower months of winter were replaced with warmer weather. At our first Spring Celebration we agreed to do some things that were different from the few downtown public events that had been held in our town before." She said, "We decided to auction off a pig, which ended up becoming a great fundraiser. And with the addition of some live music, food and entertainment, the daytime Saturday event became an immediate hit. It was the first of many more events that started bringing people to our town, many of whom had never been in Berlin before. Many people would come to one Berlin event, have an enjoyable time, and keep coming back for another of our downtown events."

Frene noted, "Friendships between downtown store owners were genuine. We purposely did not compete with each other. Downtown business owners worked to not encourage competitiveness but to be complementary. At the time our downtown did not have a lot of stores but did have a lot of variety. Some of the early events we created included the Berlin Village Fair that featured a lawnmower parade and downtown's original bathtub races. At our early Easter weekend celebrations, later rebranded the Berlin Spring Celebration, we got businesses to be sponsors of pigs and held pig races on Main Street."

This was soon followed by the annual Berlin Fiddler's Convention in late September. The original fiddler's events were organized by Jim Barrett and his musician friend Frank Nanna. "They hit the right formula immediately and with just some minor tweaking over the years it remains very popular," Frene said. The Berlin Fiddler's Convention now attracts country musical artists and fans from well beyond the borders of Maryland.

Frene said that in the late 1970s the Town of Berlin and local businesses started hosting an annual Christmas Parade. It was an instant success, attracting ever-growing crowds early each December. This evolved into Berlin's annual Victorian Christmas celebration, which attracts visitors from great distances. "It started as just a one-weekend celebration but now extends from Thanksgiving through New Year's Eve. It has become both an attraction for many visitors and great pride for the community as the festive holiday decorations have spread beyond the downtown," she added. "Taking pride in your town and what it can become is essential, that is what my dad believed. Berlin's businesses and residents developed a common belief that the more you believe in your town, the more people are going to visit and shop. Downtown has become not just a place where businesses operate, but the combination of several events, the restoration of buildings and public spaces, have all been driven by the love people have for this town."

"The transformation of downtown may be best described as a blooming of its potential. It's never too late to revitalize a town or smaller city. Businesspeople and residents must both decide if they want their town to be a thriving, working place or simply accept a long-abandoned place with empty streets." Frene added, "The potential is always there, you just have to accept that it takes lots of work. You need enough people to say we can do it. The old saying *'put your money where your mouth is'* always true when it comes to revitalizing a downtown. And it also applies to volunteering, leading, and inspiring others." Frene added, "Many downtown business owners would attend public meetings to discuss ideas to revitalize our town. But the next morning you must want these changes bad enough to get your hands dirty by turning the good ideas that were discussed into reality. You can always start out little, but every year grow by adding more to your downtown attractions and ways to welcome visitors. Know that there is always something that can be done to make things better."

Steve Frene is Debbie's husband and for many years together they owned and operated the Victorian Charm shop on Main Street. Now they are both retired. Steve was not only a downtown business owner but also was very active for several years in the Berlin Chamber of Commerce. Steve said, "Berlin is known as a safe, interesting community. You also want it to remain affordable. What brings people to Berlin is that there are things to do, places to shop and eat, it is safe to walk, everything is close at hand and convenient, and it's all located in a beautiful historic and architectural setting. This makes for a great backdrop for special events, and the attendees, with care and attention, can be transformed into customers. Businesses want successful events because they attract more potential customers to downtown."

Steve added, "The downtown businesses need an attractive, welcoming place to grow and succeed. Over the years downtown events have put Berlin on the map. New events are always welcome, but additional events are not needed as much today as they were in the town's early years of revitalization. As the downtown business community becomes more successful, owners learn to bring more potential customers to their stores by hosting activities that bring more people in the door. One good example is that The Greyhound An Indie Bookstore on Main Street regularly hosts book signings by authors. This attracts customers to the book store throughout the year." Frene concluded, "Many towns are working to duplicate Berlin's model for revitalization and attract a new level of business and visitor traffic. It's important to keep a town attractive and viable. It's possible to rise from the ashes and begin a course towards success. As a town goes through different stages of change, business and community stakeholders should openly discuss where they want to go and what new goals should be pursued. Once you have found your common attraction or appeal, it is very important for the town and its businesses to find or create something new and different. You can't rest on what you've done in the past. As your downtown moves towards greater success you must reevaluate your goals during each stage of revitalization."

Reclaiming a Peachy Past

In my community's experience, one of our most successful annual attractions is the Taylor House Museum's biggest event of the year. This is a classic example of the past helping to redefine the future. For almost one hundred years, peaches were a major agricultural product grown in our community and shipped to the metropolitan areas of the northeastern United States. It was during the heyday of this century-long heritage on July 31, 1913, that the first "Great Peach Fest" was held in Berlin.

It was hosted by J. G. Harrison & Sons, who owned the majority of the thousands of acres of local farmland that produced the annual peach crop. This gathering of 2,000 horticulturalists in Berlin was described at the time by the daily *Philadelphia Public Ledger* as a "great gathering of fruit-growers." They visited to learn about the innovative spraying method the Harrisons had developed and used each year to protect and save the annual peach crop.

But about sixty years ago, a series of repeated and severe blights brought local peach growing and shipping to its knees, and Berlin's main economic driver ceased to exist. As transportation options expanded and mobile refrigeration continued to develop and improve in the post-World War II era, the state of Georgia became recognized as the peach capital of America and has remained so ever since.

Although the economic benefits from raising thousands of acres of peaches in Berlin has long disappeared, this legacy continues to be a source of local pride. The Berlin's Taylor House Museum opened in 1986 and immediately established the Harrison Room to recognize the importance of the Harrison family's legacy. The revitalization the Taylor House not only saved the historic home, but also made it the permanent site of a community museum. It spurred the restoration of many beautiful trees and plants within the museum's downtown property on Main Street. This spirit of natural restoration continues even today as the Taylor House Museum has received a grant to create a botanical garden on the site which will feature trees, shrubs, and plants native to the area. The museum has also received a Worcester County grant to create a walking trail in the forested area of the property.

Needing a major fundraiser to make improvements to the Taylor House Museum, in 2009 some folks came up with the idea of recapturing this lost era of local history by hosting a peach festival on the museum's beautiful grounds along downtown Main Street. Even though the peaches served and sold at what is now a major town festival were not grown within our town boundaries, that did not prevent this annual celebration from becoming a transformational event not only for our community, but also throughout the region. In a matter of two to three years this tasty festival was known for all things *peachy*, but also all kinds of other local delicious foods. This combination started drawing people from throughout the Delmarva (Delaware-Maryland-Virginia) Peninsula and beyond.

Each year the festival is held on the first summer Saturday in August and the crowd flows throughout all of downtown into the early evening. The result is that what started as a museum fundraiser in 2010 has quickly expanded into an economic benefit for all downtown businesses that continues to this day. After more than twelve years, the Peach Festival is the museum's largest annual fundraiser and a major attraction for both residents and visitors. Those peaches of our town's past were reclaimed and have once again become an important part of Berlin's present-day identity and appeal. Today the Taylor House Museum's annual Peach Festival continues to grow in popularity and attendance. And the Covid pandemic initiated another meaningful transition for the Peach Festival.

Melissa Reid

Melissa Reid, president of the Taylor House Museum, said, "It was during the pandemic that the museum's board of directors decided we wanted the festival to benefit downtown businesses more. To do this, we felt the Taylor Museum should renew our partnerships with downtown businesses. We believed the Peach Festival should become one more opportunity for visitors to support the businesses who are vital to Berlin's ongoing revitalization."

Finding Your Game Changer

As was noted earlier, Berlin's game changer was twofold. First was the total restoration and repurposing in 1982 of the commercial property now known as the Renaissance Plaza, followed shortly by the complete restoration of the Hotel Atlantic. These revitalization projects not only started to significantly restore community pride but redefined the possibilities for the future of downtown.

Here are three ideas to help you find your community's game changing direction towards economic and cultural renewal.

- o   Discovering and developing a project or initiative that creates renewed community pride is essential.

○ Make sure it is something that is visual, creates positive conversation, and can be effectively promoted beyond your community's borders.

○ It should be a project or initiative that creates opportunities for people—locals and visitors—to interact, benefit, and enjoy together.

None of today's attractions and community celebrations existed when my small town started its journey of rediscovery and renewal. Remember, an important economic driver in the success of revitalizing a community is attracting guests, not just locally, but from far and wide throughout the year.

Both economic and cultural benefits are achieved over time by developing and sharing a legacy that embraces your community's past. Certainly, it is important for your community to invest in the promotion and marketing needed to reach your potential guests. But for permanent positive change, appreciative guests will continue to return not only to enjoy the local settings and events, but also to experience genuine welcoming from friendly residents and businesses.

With inspiration, planning, and follow-through, your community's potential can be realized in a relatively short time and shared with success. It is important to keep in mind as you explore this process of rediscovery and revitalization that by providing both encouragement and support, your town's best days are not in the past, but in the years ahead.

CHAPTER FIVE

Creating New Ways
to Share Your Community

S tarting a business that is created primarily to compete with an existing shop, restaurant, bar, or artistic attraction is a bad idea. If you foster duplication of businesses and offerings—and not diversity—you will be planting the seeds of your community's economic demise. Your town can offer multiple establishments as long as they do not duplicate the experiences of your residents. A real advantage of smaller towns and communities, with social pressure intelligently applied, is that you can keep Peter from robbing Paul.

By sharing in a growing economic pie, and not just dividing your town's existing business base, you discourage and ultimately minimize cycles of business turnover. Yes, there is some turnover which is part of the natural cycle of our free enterprise system, but to prosper and grow, you need more diversity, not duplication in your downtown. While encouraging and supporting diversity in businesses, it is essential to your community's success to establish a common theme, a brand if you will, for your town. This will go a long way in attracting business startups who complement, rather than duplicate, each other.

"The best part of Berlin is our small town charm and while respecting our history, we are open to change and do

not live in the past," explained Robin Tomaselli, owner of Baked Dessert Café. "Yes, people come here to enjoy a simpler time, and enjoy local history, but this is a town with up-to-date amenities." Tomaselli also noted that people visit to enjoy the backdrop of historic architecture in a setting where they can enjoy local artwork, boutique shopping, a local craft brewery, a variety of places to dine, and even farm-to-table

Robin Tomaselli

eating. She added, "I believe we truly offer something for everyone."

Brewing Up a New Tradition

As you develop your community's attractions, don't forget that some new businesses can become magnets for enhancing or expanding your appeal to visitors while also serving local residents. In Berlin's case, almost thirty years after revitalization began, in 2011 a new business opened in our community—a local brewery. There had been some initial overtures from a larger neighboring town, but Berlin's elected public servants and business leaders made a coordinated effort to invite the future brewery owner to take a good look at our community.

That entrepreneur, Bryan Brushmiller, had a general knowledge of our town's appeal but had never considered it as a serious option for the new brewery he was starting to develop. He had worked on many product and promotional elements but had not made a firm decision on the best location. Brushmiller was invited to make some personal visits to our town and meet with small numbers of local business leaders where he also enjoyed some of the downtown restaurants and bars. During these visits he experienced the same hospitality that ever-increasing numbers of guests had discovered as our town continued to revitalize. Brushmiller also found the same welcoming attitude as a potential new business owner that our town's guests had experienced for almost three decades. Within just a couple of months he made a firm commitment to open his new business in Berlin. By coordinating with the existing civic and business leaders, arrangements were made to time the brewery's grand opening in August on a day when Maryland's then-Governor Martin O'Malley could officially cut the ribbon and make the first toast at what was named the Burley Oak Brewery. The naming of the brewery was a recognition of the importance of the town's history and origin of our community's name. Both parties have benefited from the name association.

As the craft brew customer base and regional distribution increased, so did the popularity of the brewery's image and classic bar room. During its first couple of years, the brewery's location was rented. Working with the Berlin Economic Development Department and the Mayor and Council, a tax credit of $4,000 was provided to the building's owner. This was just one more way the municipality could help spur economic development.

Not long after the brewery opened, Brushmiller bought the brewery property from the landlord. The brewery operation quickly expanded and so did the bar by adding outdoor seating, a music venue, and an additional large indoor area for events and celebrations. The Burley Oak Brewery continues to grow in popularity and annually hosts several homegrown celebrations for the public to enjoy, including all the major holidays. In addition to a large regional distribution, it has won national brewing awards and Burley Oak beer is served on tap at many of our local and regional restaurants and bars.

Speaking as a former Berlin mayor and longtime community servant, allow me to address any concerns about making your community more hospitable by developing more good places to eat and drink. During its revitalization, the community of Berlin adopted an unwritten, but strongly supported policy of "no cheap drinks" for all who enjoy our town's hospitality. Our town's new hospitality venues were considered pricey when they opened on the local scene. But the benefits of this informal, but consistently followed practice, has paid lasting economic and cultural dividends.

Remember—by making your community's hospitality classy and cool, you attract guests who have the financial ability and desire to enjoy these tasteful options while enhancing your downtown's quality of life. There will be no need for an increased police presence because the above-average pricing of food and drinks will not attract those who will become troublesome or rowdy. Upscale quality and pricing will attract discriminating guests. So, your community's businesses and residents have a question to ask of themselves: Do you want to be the best you can be, or accept the lowest common denominator for your downtown? This is an important question to discuss in both the initial stages of your town's revitalization and from time to time as your community attracts more guests and businesses.

Add Eventful Enhancements

Create a sense of anticipation and excitement as you begin adapting your community for success. By exploring the possibilities for special events and festivals you begin a journey that will generate wider interests and participation from residents and businesses. There are several events, when seasoned with local flavor and pride, that can also become annual traditions and will begin to attract many visitors in a short time. Most of these guests will be people who have never before visited your community, or possibly not even heard of it. But by bringing some aspect of history, music, culture, or community pride to the core of these events, you can establish an identify for your town that will soon be reflected widely in its reputation.

Ivy Wells noted, "Without events, Berlin would not be Berlin. Each event is a living ad for our town. When visitors have a good experience they will eventually come back when they have time to shop or dine. Some of our town's events create the best days of the year for our downtown businesses."

Following are a few ways to share your community that can either establish or enhance the appeal of your downtown as you create a brand for it. Any of these events can be advanced and promoted by your region's flavor, appeal, or style.

- New Year's Eve outdoor ball drop celebration
- Town Festivals on holiday weekends that can be celebrated with parades, fireworks, live entertainment and music. These also include all the major national holidays.
- Enjoyable events based on your town's legacy
- Festivals honoring notable people from your town's past
- Restaurant weeks with in-house, curbside pickup, and carryout dining
- Taste of the Town events featuring local restaurants and foods prepared by individuals and nonprofits in your community
- Events or attractions created to appeal to children
- Classic car shows with participants from many places

Creating New Ways with Whimsy

Regardless of the format or timing of special events and festivals that you establish to enhance your town, make sure each includes a healthy dose of whimsy. This sets the tone and mood for your attractions so they can be shared joyfully with both residents and guests no matter their origin or culture. Creating types of appeal that share universal human traits is an important foundation for success.

Some of the ways local communities add whimsy to their appeal include:

- After two or three hours of outdoor music and singing, at the stroke of midnight on New Year's Eve, event volunteers drop either a decorated imitation muskrat, chicken, miniature racecar, surfboard, mounted fish, or other highly recognized symbols that are associated with your community or region.

o   During an event, hold a costume contest featuring competitors dressed in the style of a certain historical period that has some relationship or meaning to your town.

o   Host baking or eating contests that feature foods associated with the region. These can be held with a variety of local food-favorites such as cakes, pies, seafood, or vegetables.

o   An event dedicated to live musical performances by a number of groups in a genre that reflects local and regional pride and culture.

o   A children's day celebration where kids create artwork, play outdoor games, and solve puzzles. Group photos in pre-painted art cutouts are always enjoyable.

o   Ghost tours that promote or elaborate on local legends.

o   A heritage day that features crafts, traditions, clothing, displays, antiques, local historical characters, and related events.

A Festive Downtown Venue

You can transform your downtown into a great venue for festivals and events by simply closing off some streets to motor vehicle traffic for a few hours or an entire day. This can be done in coordination with traditional holidays or on dates specifically set for the attractions and events you host in your community. Indoor and outdoor decorations can be set up throughout downtown for days or even a couple weeks before the event to promote public awareness, anticipation, and excitement ahead of the celebration.

Here are some special events and festivals that have proved successful in developing destination communities.

- ○ *CRAFT FESTIVALS* featuring hand-crafted jewelry, pottery, ceramics, photography, painting, clothing, soaps, gourmet spices, kettle corn, ice cream, and other items or foods that may reflect your area's culture and tastes.
- ○ *MUSIC FESTIVALS* featuring different genres of live musical performances such as country, bluegrass, fiddlers, Dixieland, classic rock, bluegrass, or reggae.
- ○ *FOOD FESTIVALS* enable your community to transform the downtown into an outdoor café. These may be held annually or with each new season to highlight favorite local and regional foods that are enjoyed by locals and guests.
- ○ *BEER & WINE FESTIVALS* featuring local and regionally brewed beer and wines while also offering popular regional brands. The festival can be enhanced with wine tasting and food and snacks that are a natural complement for the event.

Other successful downtown events include an annual spring or fall festival. The latter can also be promoted as an Octoberfest. Or you may also wish to consider outdoor movie nights, bicycle tours starting and finishing in your town, a variety of fun festivals, or possibly antique and classic vehicles lined up throughout downtown. Some events may even be complemented by related activities in your local park.

Outdoor Rooms Offer Affordability

Your community may have one or more great ideas for special events or attractions, but no downtown building or space available to host residents and visitors. In time, a significant investment may be possible, but this is not necessary at the start. In situations like this you may have a much less costly and relatively quick opportunity to create a place in your downtown that can be a launching pad for the transformation of your community. This is possible by identifying or creating a downtown space for an Outdoor Room.

An Outdoor Room may be an open lot or space requiring some modest demolition that can be transformed into a place where locals and visitors can relax and socialize. Such spaces can accommodate multiple uses such as outdoor activities and events, displays of public art, farmers markets, musical performances, or even movie nights. Often the owner of such a lot will be open to the purchase of the property, or a lease with an option for a future purchase, as finances and circumstances allow. This is also an opportunity to coordinate the efforts and assets of a partnership between local government, a Chamber of Commerce or downtown business association, and promoters or sponsors of special events.

Even if such a space presents itself as an unsightly empty lot, it can often be quickly upgraded without great capital expense. One frugal approach would be to level and grade the property and provide for good drainage, then plant grass. To make the lot durable and to accommodate multiple uses throughout the year, open-spaced rubber matting could be installed. The installation of such open-spaced, webbed, rubber mats may also temporarily convert grass lots into additional downtown parking for special events during times when there are a large number of visitors. Such tactics can also support heavy foot traffic and temporary booths or stages while retaining the beauty and attractiveness of natural grass on the lot. These outdoor rooms will require grass mowing and regular cleanup of debris, but the initial investment is modest.

CHAPTER SIX

Community Roots Grow
Cultural Revitalization

I t is vital to begin the process of revitalization by examining your community's roots. For this can be the basis of branding in ways that can accelerate your town's transformation into a destination community. One way is to find a community that is much further along in revitalization and has already established itself as a great place for guests to enjoy. That community will very likely be in your state or region. State Chambers of Commerce and tourism departments are ready and willing to provide you with recommendations for places that have successfully achieved destination community identities in a variety of ways.

After gathering some background and online research, organize a small group of your downtown's believers to undertake either day trips or overnight stays to those places that have already established themselves as successful destination communities. In the case of my hometown, initial information-gathering trips were made in the late 1970s by a few Berlin citizens to Frederick, Maryland. Frederick is located west of the Chesapeake Bay, and roughly equidistant from Baltimore and Washington, D.C. Even though Frederick benefited from the convenience and close proximity of two major metro areas, it proved to be a good example for our small town. At that time, Berlin had a population of less than 2,000 citizens. Today, Berlin's year-round population is about 5,000, while the City of Frederick has close to 80,000 residents.

During their visits, these farsighted Berlin citizens not only toured Frederick and its downtown, but conducted interviews with several business and community leaders. Discussions were candid and meaningful. The folks from Frederick shared both accomplishments and disappointments, but the underlying message was that success had been achieved over time through persistence and commitment. Although Frederick had more overnight accommodations for out-of-town guests, its basis for success was the development of visitors making day trips to their shops, restaurants, events, and attractions throughout the year.

Admission to most attractions was free and included live music, festivals, art exhibits, holiday tours, and other special events such as an Oktoberfest that celebrates the community's German heritage. Frederick also has well-preserved architecture from the 18th and 19th centuries, proximity to Civil War battlefields, and a variety of performing and visual arts, antiques, local wineries, covered bridges, and beautiful parks. One message that came through loud and clear was that the key to becoming a successful destination community is to recognize, celebrate, and share your town's history and heritage throughout the year.

Finding a Future from the Past

During the post-World War II years, when many older downtown buildings were being razed in towns throughout America, Berlin business and property owners did not have enough money to tear down and replace the old late Victorian Era buildings that lined downtown Main Street. But they did have just enough money to cover over the original façades. This movement was widely supported because many residents and property owners were caught up in America's postwar wave of modernization for the purpose of giving downtowns a contemporary, rather than historic, look. Many downtown storefronts were overlaid with aluminum or Formstone, both coverings that were considered at that time to be modern ways to hide Berlin's late 19th century architectural style.

Only a very few downtown buildings and two local bank buildings on Main Street retained their original all-brick historic look. In a short period of time, it became obvious that the so called "modernization" of Berlin was not working. Even more downtown businesses closed, and several converted into storage units for the booming business growth that was taking place nearby in Ocean City.

Acknowledging Your Past

Melissa Reid is a native of Berlin who has a lifetime interest in the town's past. She is a local teacher and currently the president of the Taylor House Museum. Reid noted, "Local knowledge must recognize the good and the bad in a community's history. Individuals must share their diversity in a community and not be blinded by it." Berlin's earliest roots were based on a classic southern plantation. But instead of trying to hide or ignore the town's origin, Berliners began to realize they needed to acknowledge this history. Two of the leading citizens in promoting the revitalization were residents Ed and Paige Hammond, who at that time lived in an historic home named the Burley Manor, which had been one of the residences on the Burley Plantation. It had been well preserved and adapted for modern utilities. Ed and Paige both had great knowledge about Berlin's history and its transition from a plantation into a town after the American Civil War.

"During and after the United States celebrated its bicentennial in 1976 there was a big boom in rediscovering the past in communities all over America," Reid said. The transformation of the beautiful, but run-down, home of the founder of Taylor Bank, Calvin B. Taylor, is a great example of the creation and ongoing financial support for the revitalization of a local historic landmark. The structure which now houses the Taylor House Museum was originally built on Main Street in 1832. The Taylor family were the residents of the home for many years. Calvin B. Taylor served his community as a teacher, lawyer, principal, and Sunday School teacher, and as superintendent of Buckingham Presbyterian Church. He also founded Taylor Bank in Berlin and served on the Berlin Town Council for four years and also served as mayor. He died in 1932 in his home, which decades later was restored to its historic origins and reopened as the Taylor House Museum in 1981. The restoration of the Taylor House into a museum was made possible by a successful local fundraising campaign that garnered $100,000 for the project in addition to a grant from the Maryland Historical Trust.

A Harrison Family Legacy

Near the Taylor House, Harrison Nurseries was started by peach grower Orlando Harrison in 1884. The Harrison family bought even more land as the peach business prospered, and at its height owned about 3,000 acres in Worcester County. The Hale Peach had become their famous trademark by the 1920s, and the Harrison family business at that time was the largest fruit tree and nursery catalog business in the United States. During its heyday, Harrison Nurseries became a major supplier of not only peaches, but also grapes and apples. The nurseries in Berlin produced peach plants and evergreen shade trees that were shipped and distributed both nationally and internationally.

In the late 19th and early 20th century, the home and several structures owned by the Harrison family were a very short distance west from the railroad tracks and the Taylor House. These structures housed the processing and packing of peaches, tomatoes, and the plants that produce these fruits. In Berlin, the Harrison family also owned and operated both a basket factory that produced the baskets used to ship their products, and an ice plant to provide the ice needed to safely ship the locally grown peaches to the larger metropolitan areas to the north. The Harrisons soon began shipping mostly fruit, especially peaches, but also small fruit trees and seeds. The original Harrison Nurseries structures faded away in the post-World War II years.

A vital economic link in Berlin's past was having a major railroad adjacent to the Harrison Nurseries traveling north to south that made stops in Wilmington, Delaware;

Philadelphia, Pennsylvania; New Jersey, and ultimately in New York City. The railroad first came to Berlin shortly after the Civil War. A railroad station was built just north of the Taylor House in 1868. The rail hub was named Union Station and brought numerous visitors to the town for decades, including many salesmen. The salesmen would take orders from not only Berlin businesses, but from country stores throughout the area. The salesmen stayed at the Hotel Atlantic, which became the base of their local operations. The local railroad line was absorbed into the Pennsylvania railroad system in 1915 and continued to serve the town for another fifty years.

Unused for several years, Berlin's former Union Station building was purposely destroyed in the late 1960s by a controlled burn to create a location for a new Berlin Volunteer Fire Company firehouse. In 1970, a part of the old railroad station property was used for the construction of a new county library to serve the town. This public use as a library continued until the construction and opening in 2018 of a much larger county library, located just a few hundred yards up the street.

In 1995, several Berlin civic groups, churches, and the municipal government partnered to celebrate the fiftieth anniversary of the end of World War II. The celebration included a parade and the honoring of residents who had survived the war. The Taylor House Museum was central to this celebration, and it became the forerunner for many Berlin special events that would develop in the years that followed and continue to this day.

Berlin's Renaissance Begins

Joe Moore, a prominent local attorney and former Worcester County state's attorney, is a lifetime resident of Berlin and serves as the chair of the Berlin Historic District Commission (HDC). Moore said, "Key factors in the revital-

Joe Moore

ization of a town are to first create ambience by restoring the architecture to its historic standards. Also essential is to put the Main Street utilities underground, or out of view, so the preexisting and obtrusive power poles are no longer visible." Moore added, "And there was also a real need to provide interesting retail areas by a variety of businesses in town."

Moore contrasted Berlin's commitment to historic restoration to the efforts of another town on Maryland's Eastern Shore. "Up until about fifteen to twenty years ago, this other historic town had revitalized into a community of several charming retail stores and a few restaurants. This spurred the revitalization of the quaint community for many years. But over time most of those businesses have now given way to variations of what we today call t-shirt shops," Moore said. In contrast, he added, "Berlin has continued to transform but has stayed true to its historic roots by promoting and supporting its downtown businesses and unique shops that have a lot of ambience. Our town has a lot of good historic architecture. Where there used to be utility poles they are now out of sight, and today there are now many interesting shops and restaurants. The combination not only attracts visitors but gets them to stay all day."

Moore heartily agrees that the rediscovery of a town's roots is very important to any revitalization, both culturally and economically. He cited the complete renovation of Renaissance Plaza as the "first significant thing" to happen in the revitalization of Berlin. Renaissance Plaza was the first downtown restoration project in Berlin, but it was quickly followed by revitalization of a building at 18 Main Street. At that time, it was the offices of the Williams, Hammond, and Moore law firm. The firm still owns the property, but it is now leased by the very fashionable Bruder Home retail store. During the early 20th century, most of Berlin's Main Street buildings had fallen on hard times. But one of law firm partners, Ed Hammond, found a postcard that showed their location on Main Street as it looked in the 1890s. "Ed's postcard had an immediate impact on all of the firm's attorneys and they enthusiastically agreed to invest and restore the building to the architectural appearance it had enjoyed in the late 19th century," Melissa Reid noted. The results were highly visual and accelerated interest in downtown renewal, but with a return to the look and feel of an earlier time.

As mentioned earlier, returning Main Street's historic Hotel Atlantic to the elegant appearance of its heyday was a key milestone in revitalization. To start the hotel's renovation, a group of local investors put up $100,000 each for the project. These farsighted investors were: Mr. & Mrs.

James G. Barrett (James deceased); Mr. Reese F. Cropper, Jr.; Mr. & Mrs. William E. Esham, Sr. (both deceased); Mr. and Mrs. William E. Esham, Jr.; Mrs. Elizabeth Henry Hall (deceased); Mr. & Mrs. L. Clark Hamilton, Mr. Edward H. Hammond, Jr. (deceased); Mr. & Mrs. Richard G. Holland; Mr. Charles R. Jenkins, Sr.; Mr. & Mrs. William C. Mariner; and Mr. & Mrs. Alan Guerreri.

The contractor for the hotel project was Larry Widgeon, who had earned a reputation for quality restoration and resourcefulness. Several months into the hotel's renovation it became evident to the contractor that much more money would be needed to return the building to its original historic origins and at a cost that was significantly greater than the one million dollars that had first been invested.

The first challenge was to deal with a plain brick structure that had been built in the late 1940s. With a more modern, but very plain façade, it totally blocked any view of the former hotel from pedestrians and motorists on Main Street. It was constructed purposely to hide the hotel's original façade, which had never been seen by younger generations. This "modernization" addition, sadly, had, resulted in a very nondescript building concealing the historic hotel. The first step in restoring the hotel, therefore, was to completely demolish the plain brick building that blocked it from view from Main Street.

By the time the renovation of the Hotel Atlantic was completed in 1992, Berlin's downtown had started its transformation back to a beautiful historic place. The hotel, which traced its origins to 1895, was both an essential part of the revitalization of downtown and accelerated the momentum for other property owners to preserve and restore their buildings both along Main Street and intersecting downtown streets. "The return to the look and feel of an earlier era was critical to making the town attractive and enjoyable for residents. The hotel also began attracting significantly greater numbers of visitors during the late 20th century and early 21st century," said Moore, chair of the HDC, which was created to protect these early revitalization projects and to encourage other downtown property owners to proceed with the restoration of their properties.

"Prior to the late 1970s, there had not been a reason for motorists to stop in Berlin," Melissa Reid noted. This was the case even though the resort beach community of Ocean City, Maryland was just six miles to the east and began to grow exponentially after World War II. "One of the most common attractions for Berlin since physically revitalizing its past is that it now provides many places where there are opportunities to share its history, ambience, and culture," she said. Examples of such places are Rayne's Reef, the Drummer's Café in the Hotel Atlantic, Sisters Gifts & Wine Bar, and several other downtown restaurants and bars.

"Berlin's downtown is a real place and was not created as an artificial attraction," Reid said. "For most of the mid-to late 20th century there was no reason to stop in Berlin. But now, with so many more restaurants and unique shops, it's harder to find an empty parking space than at any time before Berlin's revitalization."

A Rebirth – Although the Hotel Atlantic had been restored a few years earlier, it was permanently reborn when John and Michelle Fager became the operators of this historic downtown landmark in the spring of 2009. Their work as the hotel's caretakers was immediately rewarded and continues to be the centerpiece of a revitalized downtown Berlin.

Outdoor Dining – In recent years outdoor café style dining in front of the Hotel Atlantic, on sidewalks and restaurant decks at various downtown locations has become another enjoyable attraction for both Berlin visitors and residents. It is one more example where creative adaptation is encouraged that recognizes the inevitability of change while preserving the town's historic charm.

Hotel Atlantic – The rebuilt hotel was the origin of Berlin's first rebirth following its construction after the town's first of three major fires between 1895-1904 that collectively destroyed the entire downtown business district. Private investors and the town turned this adversity into advantage that continues today.

Downtown Main Street – A great example of a community that was revitalized economically and culturally by not only renovating properties but providing the welcoming feel of an earlier time that continues to be consistently shared with people who visit or move to Berlin.

Parking With Appeal – Downtown Berlin greatly benefits from privately owned fee-free motor vehicle parking. The town provides landscaping, maintenance and plantings for the appealing landscaped areas adjacent to both parking lots and pedestrian sidewalks. There are a total of fifty spaces for motor vehicles in the largest privately owned but no-fee public parking area. And this number doubles when all other free downtown parking areas are added.

Jeff Auxer Designs – This studio filled with colorful and creative handmade blown glass on Jefferson Street was encouraged by the Arts & Entertainment designation downtown Berlin was awarded in 2005. Now 5,000 people attend Auxer's "Make Your Own Ornament" classes during each Christmas holiday season.

Taylor Bank – Founded in 1907 by Berlin resident Calvin B. Taylor, this downtown landmark is one of a very few that has maintained its original exterior look by not getting caught up in the modernization movement that followed the end of World War II. Over the decades since the late 1970s, almost all other downtown Berlin properties have returned to their original historic façades.

Main Street Berlin – Revitalized buildings all along downtown Berlin's Main Street were returned to their historic character over a couple of decades and now are filled with unique and artistic businesses, which has made this walkable corridor not only stunning and appealing, but vibrant with shoppers and visitors.

Bruder Home & Treasure Chest – Both of these properties on Main Street were among the earliest to be revitalized back to their original late-Victorian historic architectural style in the 1970s. The rediscovery and return to Berlin's downtown historic look continues to this day.

Artistic Flair – This former bank building and finance office across Main Street from the Hotel Atlantic has been refurbished into shops with an artistic flair and unique shopping. They are Life's Simple Pleasures, Dollie's Popcorn, and The Dusty Lamb. Including both adjacent buildings they are a classic example of repurposing older properties into a 21st century asset for the town.

Harrison Family Home – Harrison's Nurseries in Berlin was once the largest fruit tree and nursery catalog business in the United States. The family home known as Windy Brow was the home of Senator Orlando and Addie Harrison, and his son G. Hale and Lois Harrison. The home remains in family ownership and graces Berlin on the former Harrison's Nurseries property.

Berlin Welcome Center – Located on Main Street, the town's Welcome Center is in a highly visible and accessible place for the community's guests to get free information and advice on how to best enjoy their visit.

Plant Plaza – An open space that once served as a bank drive-thru immediately across from Town Hall has been converted into a "Plant Plaza" that provides a very colorful variety of plants and flowers as pedestrians walk along downtown Berlin.

Special Events—Your town can create a sense of anticipation and excitement by hosting a variety of special events throughout the year. They will generate interests and participation from residents and businesses and soon become annual local traditions that will attract many new visitors in a short time.

Mermaid Museum – The world's first museum dedicated solely to mermaid-themed displays has quickly become a popular draw for visitors to downtown Berlin. Here, founder Alyssa Maloof proudly displays a large seashell at the museum. Visitors are welcome to pose for photos in the seashell and a "mermaid" bathtub.

Peach Festival – Each year this festival is held on the first Saturday in August and draws overflow crowds to the Taylor House Museum. What started as an annual museum fundraiser in 2010 has quickly expanded into an economic benefit for all downtown businesses. By reclaiming peaches, metaphorically speaking, they have once again become an important part of the town's appeal.

Festival Volunteers – Ray & Kelly Thompson serve up fresh peaches at Berlin's annual Peach Festival. The annual event has become the major fundraiser each year for the Taylor House Museum and draws hundreds of people from far beyond the community.

Berlin Cruisers – An annual tradition each spring is when the Berlin Chamber hosts a classic car competition along Main Street. The event is not only popular with residents but is also a draw for visitors who also enjoy downtown shops and restaurants.

New Year's Eve Ball Drop – An annual holiday event that attracts families and guests from throughout the region is Berlin's two New Year's Eve ball drops. The first is held for families with youngsters at 6 p.m. coordinated in time with the midnight ball drop in Berlin, Germany. And a second ball drop for adults is held at midnight local time in the heart of downtown on Main St.

Midtown Offices – When areas are adjacent to an historic downtown area but are in need of redevelopment, it presents an opportunity to provide a complementary style building with all the modern technology needed for the 21st century. A successful example of this approach to revitalization is the Midtown professional center.

Holland House B&B – Jim and Jan Quick were among the early believers in a revitalized Historic Berlin and bought the Holland House property in downtown and repurposed it into a popular Bed and Breakfast. They opened the B&B in 1986 and happily have never had reason to look back.

Berlin Town Hall – The Town Hall façade facing Main Street proudly proclaims the community's status as *America's Coolest Small Town*, a title that was bestowed upon the Town of Berlin in nationwide online voting in 2014 sponsored by *Budget Travel* magazine. Also, in front of Town Hall is one of the many wayfinding signs that help downtown Berlin visitors find shopping and services.

Berlin Variety Store – The first downtown Berlin revitalization project was completed in 1981. Above is a view before the restoration of the old building, which had been covered in the 1940s with Formstone. The covering was removed and became a gamechanger for the appropriately renamed Renaissance Plaza. It soon set an example of revitalization for several other Main Street properties. *(Taylor House Museum photo)*

Sisters & World of Toys – Independently owned shops now fill locations on Berlin's Main Street that were once either national chain stores or franchises of national brands. Two current examples of the successful conversion to locally owned and operated shops are Sisters Gifts & Wine Bar and next-door neighbor World of Toys.

Tripoli St. & South Main – Kenwood was built in 1833 on the Burley land grant tract. The period home is noted for the magnificent stand of boxwoods located in the front of the property. It is believed these boxwoods were imported from England when the house was new.

The Globe & Rayne's Reef – Both located at the heart of Berlin, these historic commercial buildings now serve as restaurants. The Globe also provides live music, and both businesses are known for their hospitality. Walkability and visual charm are also common downtown attributes in Berlin's revitalized downtown.

The Odd Fellows – The Berlin Main Street property that for decades had been known as The Odd Fellows building has gone through several transformations but always has maintained its historic charm. It now serves as the location of three businesses: Gold Crafts, DreamWeaver, and the Mermaid Museum.

Dr. Rev. Charles Albert Tindley – Born in Berlin in 1851 to a slave father and a free mother. He later, as a resident of Philadelphia, became one of the most famous African American Methodist ministers of his time. He wrote the words and music for several hymns, including "I'll Overcome Someday," which is the basis for the U.S. Civil Rights anthem "We Shall Overcome." Artist Jay Coleman painted a mural in 2022 honoring Rev. Tindley on the side of the Bruder Hill building in downtown Berlin.

The Chandler House – On North Main Street across from the Taylor House Museum is one of the oldest residences in Berlin, built in 1795. The land was part of the Mount Pleasant tract and was bequeathed to Tabitha Evans in 1770. She married William Stevenson, who in his will left a half-acre for use as the Methodist Episcopal Meeting House. The Methodists named their new church the Stevenson Methodist Church, which continues its service to the community today.

Burley Manor / Burley Cottage – Two of the original residences from the Burleigh Plantation, which dates back to a 300-acre English land grant in 1677. Built in the 1700s, both Berlin homes have been very well maintained and are located on South Main Street. The plantation ultimately evolved into a village that is now the Town of Berlin. Above is the Burley Manor. Below is the Burley Cottage.

On What Grounds – Outdoor sidewalk seating is another recent addition that is enjoyed by both residents and visitors in historic downtown. This outdoor café style has been a benefit that was the result of looking for innovative solutions that also reflect the town's historic look and feel.

Wayfinding Signs – At several key locations, wayfinding signs improve visitors' experiences when they are walking or riding in downtown Berlin. These colorful signs assist the town's many guests by helping people to find parking and public services throughout the year. Placed next to this wayfinding sign on Main Street is one of several sandwich board signs that help visitors find places to shop and eat.

Two Major Gamechangers – The restoration of two properties were the early inspiration for the revitalization of Downtown Berlin in the late 1970s and early 1980s. Above is the totally rebuilt Hotel Atlantic. The original brick hotel building was built after the town suffered the first of three major fires between 1895-1904 that collectively destroyed the entire downtown business district. Below is the totally remodeled Renaissance Plaza that turned a former retail discount store into four locations for first floor businesses and three tasteful upstairs apartments.

Outten's Delights – This was the location for decades of a locally owned pharmacy on Main Street. In the 1970s it was transformed into one of Berlin's first antique shops. The growth of antique shops continued for many years and is now the location of Outten's Delights, one of three retail antique and gift shops owned and operated by Bill Outten.

Formstone – The Broad Street back entrance to the Fathom clothing boutique is the last remaining Formstone exterior in downtown Berlin. This exterior covering was widely popular in the years immediately following World War II as part of a nationwide fad to modernize.

Revitalization Success – Two Main Street businesses that represent the success of Berlin's revitalization are the Boxcar on Main restaurant and the Victorian Charm gift shop. Victorian Charm was among the earliest retail businesses on Main Street to embrace the idea of downtown as a connection to an earlier time.

Main Street Looking North – Although all of these downtown buildings are based on the late Victorian Era style when they were built just before and after the start of the 20th century, they still provide their own distinctive style and architecture.

The Blacksmith – Another good example of a unique Berlin restaurant is The Blacksmith. Tasteful appetizers, meals, and desserts, all made from the owner-operator's original recipes, are offered in both indoor and outdoor venues. This location originally served the community for many decades as the town's blacksmith shop.

Sterling Tavern – Downtown Berlin has seen the opening of a number of new restaurants and bars during its revitalization, each with its own distinctive menu. This has enhanced the town's reputation as a destination community and created a new year-round appeal that is supported by both residents and visitors.

A Remodeled Retirement – The first home remodeled in Berlin by Ernie Gerardi was on Bay Street in 2003. Since then, he has refurbished many more Berlin homes plus 36 rental units and continues to invest and improve several more properties in the community.

Taylor House Museum – The Berlin Heritage Foundation purchased, renovated, and opened the town's museum in 1986. In the first years of the 20th century it had been the home of Calvin B. Taylor, the founder of Taylor Bank. The revitalization of the Taylor House not only saved the historic home but made it the permanent site of a community museum. The restoration of the Taylor House also spurred the restoration of many beautiful trees and plants on the property. This spirit of natural restoration continues as a recent grant enables the Heritage Foundation to create a botanical garden that will feature trees, shrubs and plants native to the area.

The Robin's Nest – This home, circa 1800, is immediately adjacent to downtown Berlin and is now the home of the Lackner family. The Lackners own The Dreamweaver on Main Street and had dreamed of buying the property after opening their Berlin store. Berlin is now their home.

Returning to Roots – Two other examples of North Main Street properties that completed major renovations inside and out in order to return to their architectural roots are Viking Tree Trading and the Purnell Building. On the first floor (l to r) are three retail businesses: the Viking Tree, Gilberts Provisions, and Finally Yours.

Uptown Emporium – This historically revitalized building was formerly a furniture store. This location and the one next door were both transformed inside and out as a result of major renovations by property owner Billy Esham. It is one of many examples of the successful revitalization of downtown Berlin.

Pitts Street Treasures – Shopping for antiques has long been an attraction for visitors to downtown Berlin. The display window of the Pitts Street Treasures celebrates the town's unique dual designations as the Antiques Capital of the Eastern Shore and *America's Coolest Small Town.*

Revitalized Appeal – Once a finance office and storage area, this group of historic Main Street buildings now all complement downtown Berlin's revitalization. They are filled by (l to r) The Enchanted Tea Room, The Greyhound An Indie Bookstore, the Madison Avenue Boutique, and the Bird of Paradise.

Bathtub Race Ambassadors – One of the popular downtown summer events is the annual Berlin Bathtub Races. People line Main Street to see local entries of wheeled bathtubs with both a driver and a person to push it down the street. Above are Berlin's three Bathtub Race Ambassadors (l to r): Kenny Tomaselli, Mike Wiley and Bill Hoshal.

Farmers Market – A very popular attraction held weekly downtown on Sunday mornings between May and September where locally grown produce and natural products are sold from real farmers, plus many other Berlin area vendors.

Horse & Carriage Rides – During several of Berlin's special events throughout the year a very popular attraction is this very traditional form of early transportation. Guests are not only treated to an enjoyable ride but also get to benefit from several interesting points during this guided tour of downtown.

Island Creamery – For most of its existence the building that now houses the Island Creamery has served downtown Berlin as an ice cream shop. It was briefly a bake shop, but the business was moved to Bay Street and became the popular location of the Baked Dessert Café. The ice cream shop remains as a consistent year-round attraction for families and visitors.

Paul Williams TV – In operation for seventy years in Berlin. Now owned by the founder's sons, Williams brothers Gary (l) and Grant (r), this TV repair and rental business features a Main Street lobby that displays classic television sets and other local paraphernalia from earlier times.

Planter Wayfinding – An artistic natural approach to downtown wayfinding signs (on left) can be seen in front of the Hotel Atlantic on Berlin's Main Street.

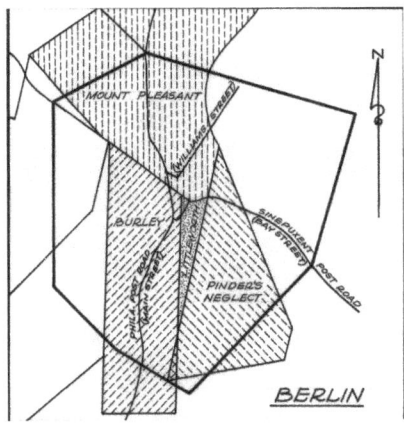

BERLIN'S BEGINNINGS – Four land grants from Great Britain were the basis for the establishment of present-day Berlin. Those grants were Burley (1683), Pinder's Neglect, Littleworth, and Mount Pleasant, all dating back to 1685. This map shows the proximity of these land grants to Berlin's Main Street (originally part of the Philadelphia Post Road) and Williams Street. *(Taylor House Museum photo)*

STEPHEN DECATUR – Born in Berlin in 1778 on a property that is now across US Route 113 from Berlin's Stephen Decatur Park, his family was from Philadelphia, Pennsylvania, and returned there three months after his birth. He entered the Navy as a midshipman and later served with distinction in our country's battles with the Barbary pirates, along the African coast of the Mediterranean. He later served in the War of 1812 and received the Navy's highest rank of that time. In 1820 he was shot in a duel of honor in Maryland's Prince George's County and died the next day. *(Taylor House Museum photo)*

THE AYRES BROTHERS – Typical of businesses in Berlin around the early 20th century was the Ayres Brothers Store on South Main Street. The building, now owned by descendant Susan Ayres Wimbrow, serves today as a tearoom and the location of The Greyhound An Indie Bookstore. *(Taylor House Museum photo)*

CALVIN B. TAYLOR – Most widely known as the founder of Taylor Bank, started in 1890, he also served Berlin as a teacher, lawyer, principal of Berlin High School, and superintendent of Worcester County Schools. He was also a member of the Maryland House of Delegates and served as a Sunday School teacher and superintendent of the Buckingham Presbyterian Church for more than twenty-five years. His home is now the location of the Taylor House Museum. *(Taylor House Museum photo)*

THE PARK HOTEL – Berlin at the turn of the 20th century was the location of a number of successful downtown hotels. Among them was the Park Hotel, which was located on Bay Street behind the location of the mayor and council offices. The classic late-Victorian style hotel burned to the ground in 1913 and was never rebuilt. *(Taylor House Museum photo)*

HOTEL ATLANTIC HIDDEN – In 1946 a plain brick addition was built in front of the Hotel Atlantic on Main Street, virtually obscuring the original façade. The hotel had gone into decline with the widespread growth of the automobile by the mid-20th century and become a flophouse. For 45 years, the plain building housed retail stores and blocked the original hotel from view until it was totally renovated and re-opened in 1992. *(Taylor House Museum photo)*

ISAIAH FASSETT – Born a slave in 1844, he was freed when he enlisted in the Union Army, US Colored Troops, so he could fight the Confederates in the Civil War. Discharged in 1866, Fassett returned to Berlin a free man. He died in 1946 as one of the longest-surviving Civil War veterans in Maryland. *(Taylor House Museum photo)*

DR. JOHN W. PITTS – (1842-1910) Served in the Confederate infantry and later under Gen. J.E.B. Stuart in the 1st Virginia Cavalry. After the Civil War he practiced medicine in Berlin for over forty years. He was a community leader and was elected Berlin's first mayor. He also served as a vice president of Taylor Bank, an elder of the Buckingham Presbyterian Church, and a district deputy grand master of the Independent Order of Odd Fellows. *(Taylor House Museum photo)*

ORLANDO HARRISON – Born in Delaware, he moved to Berlin in 1884. His family started Harrison's Nurseries, which by the 1920s had become the largest grower of fruit and shade trees in the world. He served in the Maryland House of Delegates and was mayor of Berlin from 1900 to 1908 and again in 1910. While serving as Berlin's mayor the town built its water and light system and paved its streets. *(Taylor House Museum photo)*

BERLIN'S UNION STATION – The construction of a modern railroad terminal (circa 1905) was a necessity for the growth that Berlin was experiencing at the start of the 20th century. The railroad had become the major means for passengers traveling to Berlin, including drummers, salesmen drumming up business in this region, with their luggage filled with samples of their stock in trade. *(Taylor House Museum photo)*

EARLY 20th CENTURY – In this photo, guests at the Hotel Atlantic are arriving by carriage, on horseback and by stagecoach, horseless carriages, and the new-fangled invention that soon became known as the automobile. The Hotel Atlantic provided a bus to and from the railroad station. *(Taylor House Museum photo)*

CHAPTER SEVEN

Making Your Town Artistically Alive

The artistic attributes that your town enhances or expands will ultimately develop into its cultural identity. It is this identity that will broaden your town's appeal to artists with a variety of skills that ultimately attract many appreciative guests.

Patty Backer is the owner and artist in residence at the Dusty Lamb shop on Main Street. She said, "Arts and enter-

Patty Backer

tainment in Berlin has grown so much over the years since I first started. In the early years I would have to go to Baltimore or Philadelphia to sell my art because at that time there were almost no places that would sell art in Berlin." Over time the revitalization of the town created businesses that support the arts. "As the town attracted more visitors and got busier, the shops started selling more art along with all their other goods. People now visit and look for places that show the local culture and what makes us different."

"We are really lucky to live in such a beautiful area," Backer said. "We attract people from other places because our town is near wonderful natural scenery, Assateague Island, lots of beautiful woods, and the Pocomoke River. Being so close to so many different habitats is a great place for artists." They can use these backdrops regardless of whether they are traditional landscape painters or if they use their imagination to paint creative landscapes.

"It is amazing how different our town is now, from even ten years ago. More than ever, we have people come here from all over the place. They come and find such a cute little town. And more people are saying they want to live here. That's because our pace of life is different," Backer continued. "In some ways it's old-fashioned and people often walk or ride bikes in town. People in our town are really friendly and visitors from metropolitan areas are not used to that." As the town has revitalized and rediscovered its roots, more people visit Berlin than in anytime from its past. Backer added, "Since the pandemic began, we have more visitors all year long and not just from Baltimore and Washington, but even upstate New York." She also noted that many people are choosing to drive rather than fly on airlines. "When the pandemic hit, we were initially concerned it would hurt local businesses in our town, but over time it actually brought more people than ever to Berlin."

Backer said that this has been helped by more artists moving to a revitalized Berlin. "We are just a day trip away and offer a good spot for visitors to find artwork and artists who are looking for a good place to sell."

Backer added that Berlin's many special events are good for the town in every way. The events are so much fun, and event visitors also buy artwork. "I see it only getting better with time. People love our town's diversity of shops and experiences. There are so many types of art sold here, including works by photographers, folk artists, landscape artists, and so many other types." Backer noted there are some crafts that can also be considered art. People can see artistic crafts being made and enjoy not only buying their productions, but also just watching craftspeople at work. "You learn so much about an area when you see what the local artists are creating."

Anna Mullis is the director of the Worcester County Arts Council, a private nonprofit corporation established in 1977.

Anna Mullis

The council's gallery and offices on Jefferson Street in the heart of downtown Berlin have also become an energetic force in the development of the arts throughout the county. Mullis said, "Since 2005, Berlin has made a huge step forward with more thriving businesses and people coming here from all over the place. The year 2005 was very important for Berlin. This is when the town was designated an Arts & Entertainment District by the State of Maryland." She added, "It provided more exhibiting opportunities and tax incentives for the artists, and these definitely increased the number of artists who display and sell their art here. The Arts and Entertainment District designation also increased the number of visitors coming to downtown local galleries. This resulted in an artist co-op being created so more and more artists could display and sell their art." Mullis noted that in addition to the Arts Council's downtown gallery, they have established another gallery space on the second floor of Worcester County's new library on North Main Street in Berlin.

Another significant change, Mullis said, was the establishment of Second Fridays in town. On every second Friday, Berlin shops offer extended hours and local artisans display their creations in downtown shops and, weather permitting, sell their art outdoors on Jefferson and Commerce Streets. Visitors come to town, browse, and shop in the stores and the County Arts Gallery and then many stay to enjoy dinner at one of the local restaurants.

Mullis noted that former Main Street Director Michael Day was instrumental in creating many more downtown special events in Berlin. These, coupled with the development of arts, have made the arts an economic engine for the town. They also provide an intellectual and cultural experience for visitors. "This helps the local economy and especially increases the visitors spending on the arts," Mullis said. "The next project we will be doing is a data study to measure the economic impact of the arts on our county." Initially, Berlin's Arts & Entertainment District was handled by volunteers, but as the popularity of arts and events grew, the Town of Berlin took over coordination of the program. There are ever increasing expectations for the quantity and quality of the artwork that is displayed and sold in the town.

During the extended Covid pandemic, the Arts Council Gallery was closed to visitors, but many artisans realized how much the community needed to be connected to the arts. In response, the Arts Council presented exhibits online and through YouTube. They also created a new additional website that not only exhibited local artwork but also is used for online and silent auctions. "The concept of the arts has changed over the years," Mullis said. "People not only appreciate the arts and just feel good about them, but the arts are more than just something to admire. They now recognize that they uplift people's spirits. This is not just an additional benefit that the arts provide, but they have become something essential to our lives."

"The pandemic forced us to reimagine the ways we could connect to other people," Mullis said. The Arts Council is active throughout Worcester County and provides grant funding for not only music and arts activities, but also for farmers markets and Worcester Youth and Family Counseling. They also are building more community ties by working with Worcester County Public Schools, public libraries, and with parks and recreation departments. These efforts continue to enhance support and awareness of the arts throughout the entire county. "All of this cooperative effort has made so many people, both residents and visitors, really appreciate and realize how much the arts bring to our communities," Mullis added. "We are even told that many families who visit want to move to Berlin."

Arts & Entertainment Magnets

Jeffrey Auxer Designs is a studio in downtown Berlin that makes fine artistic creations from blown glass and has been in operation for thirteen years. The process involves taking raw glass and melting it down in a furnace at 2,200 degrees Fahrenheit. The high heat turns the material into molten glass that can then be shaped and colored into three-dimensional art. The studio's owner, lifelong Berlin resident Jeff Auxer, learned the craft of glass blowing at Salisbury University.

After graduation from college, Auxer was employed by John Fager, who later became the operator of the Hotel Atlantic. When Fager and his wife, Michelle, were considering leasing the hotel on Main Street in early 2009, he encouraged Auxer to look into the Carriage House building behind the hotel as a potential location for a glass art studio that Jeff wanted to open. That property, immediately in back of the hotel, is located on Jefferson Street. In horse and buggy days, it was the place to secure the carriages of hotel visitors.

Auxer visited the former Carriage House building, but on that same day he also noticed that the building immediately next door was posted with a For Sale sign. He immediately contacted the owner and after visiting the site, Auxer bought the building as the location for his long-anticipated glass art studio. He was in the process of purchasing the building when he learned from a very old but accurate hand-drawn land plat from the 19th century that the property had once been named The Job Lot. The plat also showed that the property had been sold on September 29, 1897 to Jesse R. Gibbs. Auxer bought the building and property 112 years later from Gary Lynch on April 9, 2009. When Auxer was renovating the building into a glass design studio he found an incredible amount of old horseshoes on the property. "With its location next to the Carriage House it must have been a blacksmith shop in the old days," Auxer added.

When he first opened his glass studio there were a number of store vacancies on or adjacent to Main Street. Auxer had been very pleased and encouraged when four years earlier, in 2005, downtown Berlin was awarded its Arts & Entertainment District status. By offering special property and income tax incentives to qualifying resident artists, Auxer says Berlin's A&E District designation inspired other artists like him to locate downtown. After opening the glass design studio, he and his wife, Hilari Ashton Auxer, then added an 1,800-foot second floor to the studio building that is now their residence.

Each holiday season Auxer conducts *Make Your Own Ornament* classes at his studio and in his first year he hosted fifty classes. During the 2021 holiday season, he conducted 1,500 classes over six weeks that were attended by about 5,000 people. "When people come to our town they have something to experience and that's a big part of what makes them come back," Auxer said. "A lot of our downtown business owners are on the same page. You want every business to be as motivated and dedicated to making both our visitors and our townspeople happy to be in Berlin."

"In recent years, Berlin has become more interesting and welcoming," he added. In addition to shopping and eating, there are also more events, carriage rides, ghost tours and historic tours of the downtown. "This re-discovery of the town's history with an emphasis on art has motivated a lot of my friends who grew up in Berlin to move back and start their families here," Auxer said. "And some are also starting businesses in Berlin."

Auxer said his efforts are just one example of the entrepreneurial spirit of today's younger generation of downtown Berlin business owners. "They are willing to risk everything to fulfill their belief in their business and this town," he said. "They are not just operating a storefront but creating businesses that have made the town a destination for many visitors. By having a variety of interactive activities it makes our town a destination and not just a place to shop.

"Going backwards is always worse, but even taking baby steps is better than doing nothing at all. You should always be thinking forward, even in times when things are not changing as much as you would like," Auxer said. "Don't wait and risk letting your community become stale. Just as a family evolves, so should a community. Our town is so quaint and not only visitors, but also residents, want to support the businesses in our town. In the past six years I have driven my car no more than a total of about 11,000 miles. Everything I need is here, and I think that is one of the reasons so many people visit and want to live here." Auxer concluded, "I would not be who I am without Berlin."

Expanding Downtown's Footprint

Some of your town's new entrepreneurs will likely be folks from a variety of careers who are drawn to your small-town charm, but now have the opportunity to operate a business that has long been their dream. One such family that moved to the Berlin area and made a lasting impact is the Tomasellis.

Robin Tomaselli grew up as a resident of Olney, Maryland, just north of Washington, DC. She had been visiting the Lower Eastern Shore since she was a youngster and developed many fond memories during her visits over the years. "I always loved walking on the sidewalks of Berlin and thought the town was charming," Robin said. She had dreamed of living and working in our quaint town and her hopes became a reality.

In April 2010, Robin's Baked Dessert Café opened as a new business in downtown Berlin. Its original location on Main Street had been the Little Pink Bake Shop and before that it had been an ice cream shop. (Ironically, today that original location is once again the home of an ice cream shop called the Island Creamery.) Robin was operating a small bake shop in her hometown of Olney, when she saw a newspaper ad announcing that the little bake shop in Berlin wanted someone to take over its lease. Robin's husband, Kenny, was very supportive and knew he could continue his career if the couple moved to Maryland's Eastern Shore. So, a move to the Berlin area was a feasible and welcome idea for both of them.

Tomaselli soon formed a business partnership with Michelle Eppert and Jill Hoshal, who both shared her desire to operate a bakery in Berlin. They negotiated a lease for the space that had been the Little Pink Bake Shop. Tomaselli said they received great support and encouragement from Michael Day, Berlin's economic development director, and Olive Jones Mawyer, Berlin's director of the Chamber of Commerce. Robin, Michelle, and Jill leased the Main Street location and opened Baked Dessert Café in April 2010 on the first day of Berlin's annual Spring Celebration event.

"We were welcomed to Berlin with open arms," Tomaselli noted. There were only three popular downtown restaurants at that time: Rayne's Reef, The Globe, and the Hotel Atlantic—and just a few retail stores on Main Street. "There was business activity, but not a lot going on like there is today," she added. "The town's special events were our biggest days of the year and really brought people into Berlin and they still do." Baked Dessert was only at its original location for one year because three downtown Berlin attorneys—Ed Hammond, Joe Moore, and Ray Shockley—informed Tomaselli that a property the law firm rented on Bay Street was becoming available. "Those three men, our landlords, did everything they could to get this space remodeled and our business relocated," Tomaselli said.

Not only did the move greatly benefit Baked Dessert Café, it also expanded the footprint of downtown Berlin's business district. The proximity of Berlin to the resort community—close, but not too close—was beginning to bring more day visitors to downtown Berlin. "I had always believed that eventually the large tourist market in Ocean City would start to benefit Berlin," Tomaselli said. This trend was greatly accelerated when Berlin earned the title of *America's Coolest Small Town* in 2014 by way of nationwide online voting sponsored by *Budget Travel* magazine.

"The recognition as *America's Coolest Small Town* really helped to brand Berlin. We did not anticipate how busy we would be and have continued to be since then," Tomaselli said. "People discovered that Berlin really is a throwback to the turn of the century time of a hundred years ago. Our town is a destination that is not only a great place to visit for a day or a weekend but is also a great place to live." It was also about this time that the Town of Berlin was designated by the state as an Arts & Entertainment District. "We already displayed and sold local artwork in our café with no charge for commission," Tomaselli said. "We knew that customers enjoyed seeing the works of local artists in our shop and I think Berlin still has so much more it can do with public art.

"Ten years ago, the special events sustained us. Now, we get regular customer traffic throughout the year, but the events continue to promote Berlin and bring new people to our town from everywhere," Tomaselli said. "Arts and entertainment is here to stay in Berlin. It is a movement that is definitely continuing to draw a diverse population of visitors who also enjoy everything that is our downtown."

A Dream Comes True

Another businessperson who both lives in Berlin and

Tiffany Lackner

owns a downtown Main Street business is Tiffany Lackner. Her journey has also been greatly influenced by the community's local arts and entertainment scene. Lackner describes her store, the Dream-Weaver, as a healing shop that specializes in oils, CBDs, and handmade stones and crystals that are locally created or imported from countries around the globe including India, Nepal, Guatemala, Peru, and Ecuador. DreamWeaver also sells handmade tapestries, clothing, and bags of all types. Lackner buys her merchandise through sales representatives who travel to foreign countries and support Women's Reforming, an organization that provides health care, housing, and education for women in these nations.

Lackner did not grow up in Berlin but had always enjoyed her family's vacation home a few miles north in Bethany Beach, Delaware. Years later she opened DreamWeaver stores in Bethany Beach and just a few miles north in Rehoboth Beach. Then, in 2012, the Lackner family decided to close both Delaware beach stores and open a new DreamWeaver on the boardwalk in Ocean City, Maryland. The new store was a great fit and has been operating for eleven years at the Ocean City location. The new store kept the family very busy, and it was not until three years later that Lackner first visited the nearby town of Berlin.

Lackner said, "One of my favorite movies ever is *Runaway Bride* and I often said I would love to live in a town like Hale." This was the fictional name of the town where the movie was filmed in the late 1990s. Two years later, downtown Berlin was the location of a second feature film, filmed by Disney Studios and titled *Tuck Everlasting*. Lackner added, "I always thought that living in such a town would be the greatest thing ever. Then in 2015, a friend invited me to Berlin, a town I had never visited before. It was summer and we were standing on Main Street in front of the Hotel Atlantic. I looked around and said to her, 'This town looks like Hale in the *Runaway Bride*.' " When Lackner's friend responded that it should look like Hale because Berlin is where the classic hit movie was filmed, Lackner exclaimed, "You've got to be kidding me!"

Later the same day, Lackner took a horse and carriage ride to view the sites of downtown Berlin and was struck by the beauty and historical setting of The Robin's Nest, an historic downtown home circa 1800. "It was one of the most beautiful homes I had ever seen," Lackner said. "I immediately fell in love with the home and property, but it was not for sale." From then on, she would visit this beautiful historic home whenever she was in Berlin. "I would often sit on the porch and pray to God, just let me buy this house. I would be overcome with emotion thinking about all the times I had visited Berlin and dreamed of buying this house."

Lackner said her husband and four children, and her step-father and mother all have a great love for American history. "We had all talked about living in one home together and the Berlin property looked like the perfect spot." She continued to regularly visit downtown Berlin and it was during another carriage ride, two years later in 2017, that she saw a For Sale sign in front of The Robin's Nest. The home had not been sold because the owner had split the property into two lots with a shared driveway. "Our family decided we could overcome this hurdle by building a nice storage area behind the home and I contacted the Realtor who had listed the home." The real estate agent immediately informed Lackner that the owner of The Robin's Nest at that time had decided earlier that same day to reconsolidate the residential lots. The Lackners immediately went into action and quickly bought the property. The extended Lackner family is now sharing their dream and enjoying living together at The Robin's Nest.

A year later, in 2018, an ideal downtown retail location on Berlin's Main Street became available and the Lackner's opened a second store. The new DreamWeaver in downtown was an instant hit. "We love all of our local communities and we like working with people one-on-one all year long, not just seasonally," Lackner said. "We feel this area is such a beautiful place and supports the arts, so we are so glad we jumped on the opportunity to open a second store in Berlin."

Reflecting on my years as Berlin's mayor, I would often say at local fundraisers and art events, "The community of artists in our town do not artificially divide us, or narrowly define us, but instead reflect the best of Berlin. The appreciation of arts in our town encourages creativity, tolerance, cooperation, and ultimately shared happiness. I sincerely hope that the arts never leave our hearts or our Town of Berlin."

CHAPTER EIGHT

Leading by Example
Will Create Momentum

R einvestment begins with renewed belief in your town's future. After all—if you are not willing to invest in your community, why should anyone else? Monetary investments are certainly necessary, but just as important are the commitments of time, creative thought, and both human and capital resources. The combination of committed citizens and financial investment is the key to making all the difference in your town's immediate and long-term future.

Berlin was losing its appeal for shopping and visiting downtown in the 1960s and 1970s. But Bill Smith, a well-respected local insurance and real estate agent, became a pioneer in the community by advocating for a new direction for the town. Smith had an office on Main Street and believed something could be done to reverse Berlin's decades-long decline. Smith was an avid believer and a volunteer in trying to turn around the direction of the community. He believed something must be done and was determined to find out what that was.

As part of his efforts, Smith regularly visited state government offices and the General Assembly in Annapolis, Maryland. It was during one of those visits that he learned Maryland was beginning to award annual façade grants to restore commercial buildings to their original look. The grant also included funding to plant trees on Main Street and adjoining streets. Smith's persistent efforts in the late 1970s to get Maryland grant support to start downtown revitalization paid off. Working with the Town of Berlin, trees were planted throughout downtown. Some locations in the heart of downtown had not seen trees for several decades. Old photos from the late 19th century helped identify where new trees should be planted to bring back the Main Street charm of yesteryear. This return to the town's natural beauty made an immediate impression on both residents and visitors.

Investing in Your Town's Future

Not all community investments need to be large to make an immediate difference. Mobile phone access is now considered essential, as is broadband Wi-Fi service. But many small towns still do not have effective online service that people living in urban and suburban areas consider basic in this age of internet communications. At the turn of the 21st century, Berlin started building even greater momentum as it transformed into a destination community, but visitors had no easy or reliable access to Wi-Fi. So, after some brief consideration, the municipal government in Berlin made the investment to provide this service to anyone seeking reliable internet access while visiting the downtown business district.

In conjunction with the new Wi-Fi connection, the Town of Berlin placed signs throughout downtown to inform visitors of the free service. This access to Wi-Fi was also promoted on Berlin's downtown website. As the town's mayor at that time, I said, "We think our town's visitors and guests will enjoy and appreciate this added convenience. The mayor and council believe this is yet another example of Berlin's commitment to being a town that offers both 19th century charm and 21st century living."

Main Street business owner Donna Compher opened the Sisters Gifts & Wine Bar in 2012. She had always liked Berlin. Born and raised in Federalsburg, Maryland, she moved to Worcester County and lived in Ocean City, Ocean Pines, and ultimately Berlin. When Sisters opened ten years ago there were five spots open for shops on Main Street. Compher said, "I have seen a difference in just the past ten years. There is a solid foundation of businesses now. All available shop locations have either been filled by expanded Main Street shops or the opening of new businesses.

"The older businesses understand the importance of pre-

Donna Compher

senting and supporting the other downtown businesses. Newer businesses need to learn why working together and supporting each other is so important to the success of downtown," Compher noted. "It cannot be emphasized enough, but merchants, residents, and the Town of Berlin must work together to make this a great place to live and visit. New visitors come in every day. They are attracted here and return to experience the variety of shopping and restaurant options. And every year these visitors come back to Berlin anytime they are in the area. This is huge for all of us because it provides a great income for small town businesses and it's nice and encouraging to see new people discovering the town."

In addition to being a business owner for a decade, Compher has also been a fulltime resident for five years. She hopes the next stage of revitalization for Berlin will be to temporarily close two blocks of Main Street to vehicles from Rayne's Reef north to Stevenson's Lane for special events on Friday nights in the summer. "Each time we do this for special events it creates the festive, fun, feel and atmosphere the town has become known for."

Compher also said she is very pleased that so many Berlin families and locals enjoy downtown at special events. In the near future she would like to see downtown Berlin host wine and beer festivals with live music on Friday nights throughout the warm weather months. "Berlin's special downtown events don't keep people from socializing but just the opposite. Our events have already shown that both locals and visitors are enjoying downtown together." The revitalization of downtown has made adequate parking an issue, especially during special events. Compher believes expanding on the current special event bus shuttle service to multiple parking areas beyond downtown, such as the intermediate school, Heron Park, and the high school would greatly increase the parking spaces needed for current and future special events.

She also said Berlin's Ambassadors Stand needs to be re-energized and supported. "This is a very important free service for newcomers to downtown and benefits everyone. It is also important that all businesses and residents continue to recognize that creating and maintaining a positive vibe when visitors are downtown is critical to the past and future of the town."

"People want to support the mom and pop operations in town," Compher added. "But no one should take the success of downtown for granted. It took many years, but it must consistently be supported and promoted. Everything that is the foundation for our success is still here, but we should not forget how important all the past work and mutual cooperation continues to be for our downtown's future."

A New Revitalization Generation

Another downtown Berlin business owner, Mike Queen, was working at Rayne's Reef for former owner Max Feiler in the years just after 2000. It was at that time Feiler suggested that Queen lease the business from him. After some consideration Queen, at only age 19, took over the lease for the Main Street café on August 16, 2004. Queen was a member of a new generation committed to con-

Mike Queen tinuing the revitalization of downtown Berlin. "At first I was just trying to make some repairs and improvements to the building and be cost effective," Queen said. "But I knew that whatever work that I had done should have Berlin's historic look."

One of the most dramatic changes was the elimination of the old Formstone that had covered the exterior of the Rayne's Reef building for decades. "The Formstone was actually making the building less stable and was starting to fall down. I put up a brick exterior and tried to finish everything so it would all be historic, including replacing the two-story porch on the corner of the building. But I did not replace the old-style awnings because I could not find anyone who could do that kind of work," Queen said.

Operating as a downtown entrepreneur for almost two decades has only made Queen a bigger believer in Historic Berlin. "Visitors are drawn to town year after year because it is beautiful and many say they want to move here," he added. Queen says that the interaction downtown businesspeople have with visitors is critical to the success of Berlin. "They are the face of the town. How they talk to people and treat them is very important in having them come back." Queen also said the town's special events are very important in getting more folks to discover and return to Berlin. "They come to our town, walk around and discover all the stores and places to eat. As long as our visitors are welcomed, the town will just keep growing." Queen also said renovations, sometimes even when modest, will remain ongoing.

Queen noted that when a business is operated with respect for the town's historic past, it is better for all other business owners. "I know that when John Fager took over the Hotel Atlantic right across the street, I was concerned," Queen said. "But it didn't hurt. Instead, it helped my business," as even more people were attracted to the revitalized historic downtown. "When I was younger, I never thought to come to Berlin to eat. But it now has a lot of variety and that is so important. It's just not good anywhere to have a lot of the same thing. The more different and really good places you have, the better."

Currently another highly visible Main Street property across from Rayne's Reef is undergoing a major renovation. The building with three storefronts is owned by Jack Burbage, whose father, John Howard Burbage, Sr., was Berlin's longest serving mayor for 26 years, from 1962 to 1988. The Burbage building is now being totally renovated inside and out. "This will bring in more good businesses and keep the town's revitalization moving forward," Queen added.

A Downtown Toy Story

Olga Kozhevnikova was born in Russia but is now happily a citizen of the United States. While growing up in Russia, she earned a college teaching degree in math and physics.

Olga Kozhevnikova

Later she also earned a college degree in accounting. Olga first worked in the USA during the summer of 1997 and returned to America to become a permanent citizen in 1998. She worked at a variety of jobs in those early years. But in 2011, as the beach season was coming to an end, Kozhevnikova was working in a pizza shop in Ocean City, Maryland, and her hours were cut. At that time

Olga, with her work experience and education, was encouraged by a friend in real estate to open her own business. "I took a course at Wor-Wic Community College on how to start your own business which included several topics including accounting, advertising, and many other details of running a store." The first decision was determining what kind of store it should be, Kozhevnikova explained.

Her daughter was just one year old and Olga remembered how much children enjoy toys. "So, I also bought a book titled *How to Become a Toy Store Owner* and really studied it." At that time Kozhevnikova was also hearing that business activity was growing in nearby Berlin and she began looking for a location and found a small retail shop space available downtown. Olga then went to Michael Day, Berlin's Main Street director at that time, and he suggested she look into the location of what had been Toy Town Antiques, which was closing. "I immediately visited the store and soon signed a lease," Kozhevnikova said. She put what she had learned to work and opened the World of Toys on Main Street in May 2012. "I also heard about a large toy trade fair, attended the show and placed orders for my new store." Business was very slow at first and when people visited her toy store, many customers said they had never shopped in Berlin before but liked what they found.

It was also in the spring of 2012 that Kozhevnikova took a Small Business Administration (SBA) course and loan. Because of her efforts to open a new business downtown, she was asked to speak before a local SBA class. Olga told the story about her journey towards opening a business. Inspired by her example, SBA went on that year to assist in the opening of a couple more new businesses in downtown Berlin. In the years prior to Kozhevnikova opening the World of Toys Berlin had developed a reputation for having several antique stores, but a limited number of other types of retail stores. "At that time only one Main Street business, Victorian Charm, was advertising on a regular basis," Olga said. Shortly afterward, more retail businesses not only started to open in downtown but also began to advertise and promote shopping. Berlin's growing retail businesses worked together in an effort to revitalize the town's Chamber of Commerce. While downtown businesses were finding a collective voice, Kozhevnikova worked to appeal to people of all ages with a wide variety of tastes who would come in to buy toys. She stocked many toys from throughout the United States, but also from Italy, Germany, Ukraine, Denmark, the Czech Republic, Canada, and England.

Olga operated her growing toy business at the original 800-square-foot location for five years. But when a 4,000-square-foot retail space across the street became available, she jumped on the opportunity and moved her business to the new location in 2017. "To grow a business you must work hard, follow the hours of operation you post, and listen to your customers' requests," she explained. "A lot of our customers come from other places like Annapolis, Maryland, or Dover, Delaware. Over the years, customers now come from all over the place." Like other retail businesses, her store benefits from some of the town's special events held downtown. Kozhevnikova noted, "We are especially busy for the town's Christmas tree lighting on Black Friday and Small Town

Saturday the next day. We also see increased business from the sidewalk sales, and the Octoberfest celebration in the fall."

A Remodeled Retirement

Ernie Gerardi originally lived in Montgomery County,

Ernie Gerardi

near Potomac, Maryland. Then in 1988 he and his wife bought a second home in South Point, just a few miles east of Berlin. "When we bought that second home we had no idea that we would retire there," Gerardi said. "But that's just what we did in 2001." After settling into their home for retirement, Gerardi was looking for something to do that would be productive and that he would enjoy. "In 2003 I started remodeling a home on Bay Street in Berlin," he explained. "When I finished that project I bought the house next door and remodeled it," he added.

"My wife did not want to live on the water, so I then bought the house immediately next door to the first home I had just remodeled," Gerardi said. "I remodeled that second home and moved in eleven years ago and have never looked back." He added that the original home he reconstructed in Berlin is now the residence of his grown children. When Gerardi had first retired he had put all his investments into the stock market, but he decided to get out of stocks and bonds and reinvest it into fixing up homes and buildings in Berlin.

"I started out buying rundown homes on key streets coming into the Town of Berlin. I bought properties with high visibility and as each one was remodeled it would inspire other people to reinvest in their homes," he said. This voluntary process of investment and remodeling by Gerardi and other nearby property owners "got rid of a blight that had been seen for years by people coming into town." He added, "I did one home on Williams Street and as soon as it was finished the property owners on both sides fixed theirs up."

Gerardi also made commercial investments in downtown Berlin. He bought three properties on Main Street. Gerardi noted, "When I bought the old hardware store on Main Street, I had no idea of what I would put in there and after remodeling it became a high-end antique store. Then I bought the building and renovated it into a restaurant that is now Boxcar on Main which has brought more visitors into town." The third Main Street property he purchased was an old rooming house that had been closed a long time. "The building was horrible looking, so we went to work and also renovated it into a restaurant," he said. That restaurant is now the popular Sterling Tavern.

Gerardi now owns a number of residences in town plus thirty-six rental units. "I am working on remodeling five more properties right now," he added. In spring of 2022 he was also renovating a downtown home on Jefferson Street directly across from the Berlin Commons public space. Gerardi said what made him a believer in investing in Berlin was, "The town had made a change. It was willing to approve reasonable growth. It has always been my intent to help Berlin get a better image. I retired needing something to do, and I have made all of my investments since then in Berlin. My wife and I love living here. We can walk to the downtown businesses and restaurants. It provides us with a different kind of living and its image is much better."

Uncontrolled sprawl has left a legacy of destroying many communities and also undermines the viability of downtowns. Gerardi shared his expectations for Berlin's growth by the mid-21st century. "I am hopeful that the town can stay focused on what has made it a great place to live. You must have controlled growth, but you must not let growth die to maintain this town's vitality," Gerardi said. "Look around all over the U.S. and you see how small towns have died. With our location near Ocean City, we have constant exposure to new visitors and tourism. They love our hometown feel and we should keep growing at a reasonable pace." He added, "It is a friendly town that you can enjoy. For a community to have a future it must be welcoming, and for it to remain viable it also must have a downtown business area that is vital.

One of the reasons downtown Berlin continues to be a vital commercial and cultural area is it has a tradition of being welcoming to minority-owned and operated businesses. Jesse Turner started working as a shoeshine boy right out of high school. He then learned the trade of shoe repair very well and ultimately bought the business, the Berlin Shoe Box. He operated the shoe store on Main Street for 68 years with pride and friendliness until 2017 when he retired. Downtown Berlin currently has four minority-owned businesses on Main Street. They are Una Bella Salute, Madison Avenue Boutique, Main Street Nails and the Finally Yours hair salon. They are also relevant examples of Berlin's strong foundation of welcoming people from all regions, races, and places.

CHAPTER NINE

"Doing Nothing Is Always the Wrong Thing to Do"

"**D**oing nothing is always the wrong thing to do," said Lisa Challenger, the tourism director in Worcester County, Maryland, for more than thirty years. "Without revi-

Lisa Challenger

talization, you risk losing a really big piece of your past. It's heartbreaking to see old buildings being torn down instead of being renovated. The effort and investment should be made to make a town once again beautiful and thriving. Don't let people say you're crazy for believing in your town. It's a love and belief in your town that refuses to let it die. You shouldn't be embarrassed about believing, but use it to make something happen and do something about it."

Successful Places Serve as a Stage

The "Project for Public Spaces" (PPS) enables U.S.-based nonprofits and government agencies to address unequal access to public spaces by working directly with local stakeholders to transform existing public spaces or create new ones. PPS has been successfully encouraging communities to create great public spaces in several ways since its founding in 1975. PPS defines great public spaces as "those where celebrations are held, social and economic exchanges occur, friends run into each other, and cultures mix. When these spaces work well, they serve as the stage for our public lives." PPS has found that to be successful, public spaces generally share four qualities: they are accessible, people engage in activities, the space is comfortable and has a good image, and it is a sociable place where people meet and enjoy each other when they come to visit.

PPS recommends that citizens take a fresh look at your town and see what spaces can be transformed into public gathering places. This may be as simple as temporarily blocking off downtown streets to motor vehicle traffic or reimagining leftover or unused spaces into attractive and appealing places for locals and visitors to gather. PPS has identified a few basic things that can be very helpful in transforming spaces for public gatherings.

First, a successful public space is easy to get to and get through. Ask yourself: do people have to dart between moving cars to get to the place, and do sidewalks lead to and from adjacent areas? Another consideration by PPS is whether a space is comfortable, presents itself well, and has a good image; all three are key to the success of a public space. They have found that comfort and image encourage people to stay and even take pictures. They also understand that if "vehicles dominate pedestrian use or prevent them from easily getting to the space, those vehicles must be alleviated from an area used for special events to be a successful public space."

They also note that people of different ages should feel comfortable using a public space and socializing should feel natural. Sociability becomes the ultimate goal. PPS says, "This can be a difficult quality for a place to achieve, but once attained it becomes an unmistakable feature. When people see friends, meet and greet their neighbors, and feel comfortable interacting with strangers, they tend to feel a stronger sense of place or attachment to their community."

A Synergy of Energy

In the early years of this century, it was acknowledged by both businesses and town government that someone was needed who could provide community leadership and coordi-

Michael Day

nation to take Berlin's revitalization to the next level. As a result, Michael Day, a resident and former Salisbury, Maryland, City Council member, was hired in 2005 to be a shared contract employee between two towns in Worcester County. Day said, "I started as an economic development circuit rider spending twenty hours per week in Berlin and an additional twenty hours per week in Pocomoke City," a town about 30 minutes to the south.

Day explained that in both towns a major challenge in the beginning was getting an adequate number of people on board representing businesses, merchants, and government officials. Once this was accomplished, and by being hired as a contract employee, Day could also work with each of these communities' mayors, department heads, and public safety officials before starting a new initiative downtown. "In a relatively short time by adding downtown businesses and others who wanted to see their towns revitalized together, we became an extended family," he added.

"It was easier and more productive for me to have one-on-one meetings. Overcoming skepticism is necessary in such an effort. But having someone who also served as the official downtown Main Street manager was essential in developing trust between economic development and key individuals and groups in town. Unfortunately, with the start of the great recession in 2008, Pocomoke City saw the loss of some downtown businesses," Day said. "Where there had been a willingness before to change and try new things to benefit that town's economic future, with the recession, it gave way to despair and pessimism."

Berlin's response to the economic recession was just the opposite. When Day was able in 2009 to double his hours, Berlin's municipal government extended his contract to full-time. To raise money for the promotion of downtown shopping and events, Day created a Marketing Co-op with several merchants putting up first $100, then $200, and ultimately $400 each summer. The co-op now includes merchants, the town government, the Berlin Chamber of Commerce, and nonprofits. The money raised through the downtown marketing co-op was matched by both the Worcester County government and Maryland's Department of Housing and Community Development (DHCD). The combination of these three sources of funding was used to sell and promote Berlin far beyond its borders. "We did not give up when tougher economic times came. Instead, this challenge was used as a catalyst for us to pull together," Day noted.

"I was able to recruit co-op members by hosting weekly Monday morning coffee gatherings. This routine soon became year around and I was able to get many good suggestions from the owners and representatives of the co-op," Day continued. "One of the ongoing discussions was the sharing of ideas about how business and property owners in the downtown could make their shops more attractive, inside and out." Day noted that early on in these discussions, "We decided to not go after big businesses or any type of chain stores. Our direction was to get more mom-and-pops on board and support the redevelopment with a variety of downtown shops."

Day added, "The idea was not to duplicate business and create greater competition, but to expand the types of shops and amenities that would attract more visitors and add to the ambience of downtown." This effort included not only shops, but also encouraged the opening of art studios and galleries. The result of the continued discussions and support for the Main Street Marketing Co-op created what Michael Day calls "a synergy of energy" for the revitalization and continued renovation and promotion of businesses in downtown Berlin.

In the years since, cooperation between downtown Berlin, the state, and county governments has continued to grow. Economic Development Director Ivy Wells said downtown businesses have also benefited from Main Street Improvement Grants which included funds for the Wayfinding Signs and new trash cans on Main Street. The emphasis on marketing downtown has continued to grow with support from the Worcester County Tourism Department. This has resulted in more funding for Berlin's marketing outreach and regularly promotes the five months of Berlin's Farmers Market and the annual Christmas holiday season events.

Rediscovering Your Roots

Billy Esham was another property owner who played a role in the ongoing rediscovery of the town's historic roots. He understood the importance of a revitalized business district based on the town's historic past and architecture. He and his wife, along with his father and mother, Mr. and Mrs. William E. Esham, Sr., were among the eighteen investors in the reconstruction and revitalization of the Hotel Atlantic on Main Street.

Other residents and property owners also saw a growing belief in the benefits of downtown revitalization. The common goal these people shared was not to modernize downtown, but to rediscover and support the town's late Victorian Era appeal, both in support of independent businesses and the ongoing revitalization of the downtown's architecture. About twenty years after Berlin's initial revitalization, Esham and other downtown property owners continued to actively support these efforts with ideas and investment.

Bathtub Races Begin

One early example of cooperation between the town government and the private sector was the promotion of a beloved, homespun event known as the Bathtub Races. For many years on a summer Saturday, a few businesses participating in the annual Berlin Heritage Festival parade put in entries of wheeled bathtubs with both a driver in the tub and a person to push it down the street. But that single popular aspect of the parade was expanded and reinvented into its own event, an annual Bathtub Race competition, and was moved to a summer Friday night. Many entries competed in a number of heats until the two semifinalists raced for the first-place trophy.

Some of the bathtub entries were built for speed, but others featured whimsical costumes and decorations appealing to family members of all ages. The number and variety of downtown events has spread and evolved over the years and are now a regular feature throughout the entire year. Day noted that former Berlin Town Administrator Tony Carson saw the potential of downtown events and was on board in helping to create more. "When an event was not as well attended as we thought it should be, we would just keep tinkering with it or, in some cases, scrap it, or just make it another part of an already popular downtown attraction," Day said.

Day added that it is essential to have a chairperson to organize and champion each event. Different events will likely have different chairs, but they are all backed up by the town's economic and community director and staff. Almost all downtown businesses remain open during these events. Most benefit financially from the special events which bring so many visitors to town, but not all benefit equally from every event.

Day noted that one great example is that Terri Freeman Sexton, the owner of the Treasure Chest, a multigenerational Main Street jewelry store, remains open for every special event downtown. "One event may benefit her very little, but others doubled her sales. She has always been sure to stay open during all downtown events, not just those that she benefited from financially." Day notes that this attitude and approach has done much to bring back event visitors at other times, ultimately benefiting Main Street merchants throughout the year.

Quality Over Quantity

"One of the basics required to revitalize a downtown," Day said, "is to hire a paid Main Street coordinator." Initially you may have to start with someone part-time. In Berlin's case, after a couple of years, these efforts evolved into a full-time Main Street coordinator." In Day's experience as the director, he had many discussions with downtown revitalization supporters. He handpicked people to serve on each committee who had a common desire to see Berlin flourish based on its revitalization and history.

One constant maintained throughout this revitalization process was an absolute emphasis on quality over quantity in all things. It still is a very important criterion as this process continues. Sometimes success is based on nuances in the way a community presents itself. In Berlin's case, as economic activity increased, so did the trash generated in downtown. To offset this and maintain a clean and inviting look, the town more than doubled the number of trash cans in the downtown area. Those trash cans now have a special color that blends in with the historic architecture, and sport logos with the town's designation: *America's Coolest Small Town.*

"A key factor that has continued the revitalization process is not to keep doing the same thing over and over without benefiting from different results," Day said. Among those factors is a willingness to help financially support group-paid advertising; a widely promoted downtown webpage that is regularly updated; and a willingness to change or completely replace an event that is fading in attendance.

From his own experience, Day advised everyone to overcome skepticism about new strategies and events. Especially in the beginning, believers in a downtown need to develop a thick skin towards criticism and doubters. "Despite the critics," Day said, "just keep doing what is working and realize that sometimes you have to shut down things that are not working." A very important accomplishment for downtown was when Berlin was designated as a Maryland Main Street community. "You were required to host three signature events in a year plus one smaller event every month," Day said. "Any downtown that aspires to become a better place should practice the principles of the Main Street program," he added.

Although now retired, Michael Day is a member of the Worcester County Tourism Commission. As a tourism volunteer, he maintains and resupplies the county's tourism kiosk at the Salisbury Regional Airport. The kiosk is regularly resupplied with a county brewing guide, two birding brochures, and a cycling brochure. Another guide at the kiosk promotes attractions and sites in the 1999 filming of *Runaway Bride*. This very popular romantic comedy starring actors Julia Roberts and Richard Gere continues to bring new visitors to the town.

A Main Street Blueprint

Berlin's current economic development director Ivy Wells noted the importance of having financial investments follow the belief in the potential of a destination community. "Without any investments in your downtown you are guaranteed a zero return on zero investment," she said. Wells noted that at each phase of Berlin's revitalization investments have been made to turn the vision for the future into a reality. The largest investments are made by downtown property owners, but local, county, and state government must all do their part financially to be sure public amenities are available and up to date for a town's growing base of visitors.

Wells explained that her department's efforts are supported by four key volunteer committees. They are based on ensuring that at no time is any aspect of the ongoing revitalization process adrift or ignored. Wells said the four committees of the Main Street Blueprint are: 1) Promotion, 2) Economic Development, 3) Design, and 4) Organization. "All are important," Wells noted, "but it is the organization committee that gets volunteers for downtown events, to staff the Welcome Center, and downtown fundraising. It is the glue that holds all the other committees together."

▨ Return of a Beating Heart

After the Hotel Atlantic was renovated in 1992, there was a brief renaissance of guests and locals at this Main Street centerpiece, but a few years later new operators tried to change its appeal by removing many of the historical furnishings and paintings on the property. "They tried to make it a place that would be a fit for New York City or Washington, D.C.," explained John Fager. But that approach was not popular with either guests or local residents and the hotel closed on New Year's Eve 2008. That's when John and Michelle Fager took a close look at the possibilities of taking over the operation of the hotel. John had many years of experience in the hospitality business in Ocean City operating both Fager's Island and the Lighthouse Club Hotel, both on the bayside of the resort.

At that time Michelle drove through downtown Berlin on school days as she took their three children to and from

John Fager

Worcester Preparatory School on South Main Street. "She loved the historic look of the outside of the Hotel Atlantic but could see how it was not meeting its potential," Fager noted. "Michelle had a lot to do with our interest in taking over its operation. After it closed, we looked over the property and found that the previous operators had stored away artifacts and everything that gave the Hotel Atlantic its historic appeal."

John said it was depressing to see, but the Fagers believed they could return it to the historic look and feel that it was meant to have. John and Michelle signed a lease to operate the hotel, restaurant, and bar in January 2009. With the help of staff from their Ocean City hospitality businesses, they immediately went to work putting Berlin's Main Street hotel back to the way it was when it had been restored.

The couple worked feverishly so that just three months later, in March, they were able to reopen the Hotel Atlantic to wide acclaim by providing great food, a super-friendly atmosphere, and the look and feel of an 1895 downtown landmark. "When we reopened the hotel there were still a number of business locations in downtown Berlin that were not occupied, but all that was about to change. This is the beating heart of Berlin," Fager said. "Michelle and I love being here. We are the Hotel Atlantic's caretakers, and it is our responsibility and pleasure to make sure the hotel is healthy, happy, and respected."

CHAPTER TEN

Proximity Makes for Lasting Success

One of the key factors of a community's potential as a destination community is its proximity to visitors either seasonally or year around. In this case, proximity is meant as a measure of distance, time, and the relationship you develop with your guests. The marketing and brand you identify for your community will be very important in determining which people are attracted to your destination.

Making your community a place for visitors to enjoy and support commercially while not undermining the very attributes that attract them is within your control with both foresight and planning. You need to understand why people may be attracted to visit your town. One trend during and since the pandemic is that more travelers are looking for great places to visit that are relatively nearby and do not require transportation by air or sea. Successful destination communities know their visitors (guests) are looking for more relaxing and enjoyable experience than they ordinarily find in their metropolitan or suburban homes. Communities offering respite and renewal know their visitors are seeking an alternative experience from the hustle and bustle of their daily lives. These visitors want to enjoy a long weekend, a few days from home, or are just passing through as they travel on vacation.

It can be the common desire of your community's visitors to enjoy your town while not bringing with them the intense experiences of more populated places. This can be one of the natural outcomes of your community's marketing when both the message and the audience are targeted for mutual benefit. It is advantageous for your community to not be too close to a highly populated metropolitan area. Being too close usually does not foster the development of a more relaxed and human-scale environment. Often successful destination communities are between an hour to a day's driving distance from highly populated metro areas. This enables not only a less frenetic lifestyle but is critical in encouraging and developing a local culture supported with openness and friendliness.

An enjoyable destination community is one that finds a good balance between accessibility to travelers without becoming overwhelmed by traffic congestion. Such communities also welcome and adapt to the economic benefits of visitors without losing the very cultural appeal and less intense living that make them great places for residents to live and guests to visit. The balancing of proximity and lifestyle appeal is at the heart of creating a destination that is not just a temporary attraction that fades like a fad but becomes a place for lasting success.

The short distance between Ocean City and Berlin did not significantly benefit our small town for many years, in part because there was no signage directing motorists into Berlin on either US 50 (the east-west access highway) or US 113 (the north-south access highway) to town. Ironically,

Federal Highway Administration (FHA) policy prohibits such directional signs for Berlin due to the configuration of both highways, which mark the northern and eastern boundaries of the town. But as result of the support and efforts of the Maryland Department of Transportation and State Highway Administration, signage now exists to inform motorists of entrances and exits to Berlin from these federal highways. With the support of the Worcester County Commission the state issued permits for two road signs informing motorists on both highways that they are approaching our town. The signs read, "Welcome to Berlin, *America's Coolest Small Town*" along with a second that states, "Please Slow Down In Our Town." It is also the hope of town residents and businesses that motorists will also slow down their pace of life a bit while they are in Berlin.

Donna Compher, owner of Sisters Gift and Wine Bar on Main Street, noted, "I know our business has seen a difference in just the past ten years. Our yearly income has steadily increased. And downtown has a nice variety of shops. For many of our visitors it's their first visit here in Berlin. They have traveled to Ocean City for years, but then they hear about our town and stop in to see what it's all about. Our proximity to Ocean City is very important. The town and the county have done a great job promoting our town," she added. "Many visitors hear about Berlin while visiting Ocean City, lower Delaware, and Virginia's Eastern Shore. They keep coming back because they are attracted to a town where all the businesses are not the same. They are attracted to our downtown and return often to experience the variety of shops and restaurants. Visitors don't want to find a lot of duplication."

Hotel Atlantic operator John Fager said the community's proximity to Ocean City has also provided an important advantage. "All of the local people in the Berlin area made money on the beach and brought that money to this town," Fager said. "Over time they made possible not only the complete renovation of the Hotel Atlantic but other improvements to downtown." He added, "You need both, the infusion of investments and the tourists." Fager agrees that many visitors stay in Ocean City sometimes four to five times before they discover downtown Berlin. "They read a local newspaper or they hear good things about Berlin during their visit at the beach. And they are only six miles, or about six minutes away. The proximity of Berlin to Ocean City and the beaches is a huge benefit. It gives businesses here the volume of people you need," Fager said.

"We encourage visitors to come to Berlin for a different experience," he noted. Fager said many of the hotel's guests feel like it is a little museum where they can relax and enjoy. "They can also visit the downtown shops, enjoy the view, and see how people lived and experience life like they are going back in time. Visitors in Berlin can order ice cream, root beer floats, and visit art studios." He also noted the Hotel Atlantic shares the appeal of the Shore through cross-promoting with businesses in Ocean City.

Enjoying Guests Without Gridlock

Don't allow your downtown to be overwhelmed by motor vehicles. High levels of traffic and congestion diminish the quality of life wherever they occur. With planning and the help of partners, you can anticipate and accommodate greater numbers of visitors as you transform into a successful destination community.

Jay Bergey is a certified public accountant who owns Berlin business properties. Bergey says he does not charge for parking in his downtown Main Street properties, "because I basically want to support the town and the business community." Back in the 1950s through the 1970s, an Acme Food Market was operated on Berlin's Main Street. But after Acme closed, Bergey bought the property, which included lots on both sides of Main Street. "There are a total of fifty spaces and there is no other place in downtown Berlin with that much parking," Bergey said. He maintains both parking lots privately and requires no assistance from the Town of Berlin, except for the rarely necessary removal of snow in winter. Bergey noted that Berlin's first economic development director, Michael Day, successfully applied for funding and created landscaped areas with trees and plants where the two parking lots align with Main Street. "I want no compensation for the parking spaces, but just want to help support downtown," Bergey said.

Terri Sexton, a lifelong Berlin resident, has owned and operated the Treasure Chest jewelry shop on Main Street since December 1999. She bought the business from her father, Bill Freeman, who retired that year. Sexton had worked at the Treasure Chest several years before and had always been very active in promoting the downtown business community. She and other downtown business leaders worked to revive the Berlin Chamber of Commerce, which had become inactive. Sexton, along with Roxanne Williams, a downtown bank manager; Reese Cropper III, a Berlin insurance broker;

and Jesse Turner, the owner of the Berlin Shoe Box retail store, were a group that became the driving force in revitalizing the Berlin Chamber.

Sexton noted that reasonable proximity must also be complemented by awareness. "We have the advantage of having Ocean City in our backyard," she said. "Our proximity is very helpful, but people are also attracted to our town because they have heard about one of the many awards or designations downtown Berlin has received over many years. Berlin businesses regularly send people to other people's downtown stores and it surprises shoppers," Sexton said. "But although they are surprised, they appreciate it very much." She added, "When visitors come to Berlin to shop, they end up walking around and they admire the town. Our Main Street and the downtown shops give people a feel of an old town from an earlier time."

Sexton said downtown businesses sought ways to improve the visitors' experience and this included working with the Chamber of Commerce and the Town of Berlin to create and place wayfinding signs throughout downtown. These signs help people find parking and public services and assist the town's many guests during special events. When alternative parking is needed, temporary signs direct downtown motorists to parking areas at the local parks, the Berlin Volunteer Fire Company firehouse, and nearby public schools.

For special events and high-volume weekends, we began to borrow buses and trolleys to transport visitors to and from downtown between designated satellite lots. In Berlin buses are provided by a casino located nearby. The town also uses church parking lots in and around downtown. On weekends school lots not only can provide motor vehicle parking but also can serve as pickup and drop-off locations for visitors traveling by bus or trolley to downtown.

As a result of Berlin's longstanding policy of never charging fees for downtown parking, a majority of the town's visitors enjoy downtown during daylight and the early evening. Most of the town's special events are held from 10 a.m. to 4 p.m., or 1 p.m. to 6 p.m. When the special event is over, some visitors do not want to leave, so they stay to enjoy one of our many downtown restaurants.

Setting the Stage for Success

When you block off vehicle traffic on a major downtown street, it is often useful to place performance stages or other large venues at the location of the barrier. Complemented with other public safety barriers and visual warnings, these portable stages guarantee that no motor vehicles will accidentally drive into the crowds. You should include solid backdrops and ceilings on the portable stages to brand the event and add decorative décor and lighting. The area of the street immediately in front of the stage then becomes a great place for seating.

In Berlin, we often locate a stage at both ends of Main Street. The rear of each stage blocks off vehicular traffic for safety. Having two venues also allows for performances to be scheduled at different times for each stage. This ensures that the majority of people are able to see and enjoy all the attractions as well as the businesses located along Main Street from one end of the event to the other. As the events grow in popularity, intersecting side streets can be used for expansion, but again with traffic barriers to prevent motor vehicles from encroaching on the pedestrian-only space. Temporary signage in and around your community will enable motorists to find the places you have set up for event parking. In coordination with your state highway department, both traditional and electronic signs can be used to guide newcomers to your downtown for events or festivals.

Partnering to Ensure Safety

Creating a partnership with your local law enforcement agency is absolutely necessary to ensure the safety of motorists

Arnold Downing

and pedestrians. Police officers can patrol key intersections to enhance pedestrian safety and direct motorists to your town's parking. Berlin's police chief, Arnold Downing, began service with the Berlin Police Department in 1999 and was promoted to chief in 2002. Today, he is the longest-serving police chief in Maryland. During his tenure he has been named to the board of directors of the Maryland Municipal League, the State Police Executive's Association, and the Maryland Police Training and Standards Commission.

"With special events, everything we do is a partnership. We work closely with the sponsor of the event, town public works, the State Highway Administration, and other local police agencies," Chief Downing said. The Berlin Police

Department provides mutual aid with other police agencies and regularly works with the Maryland State Police and Worcester County Sheriff's Office. The chief noted that years ago most special events were held in Stephen Decatur Park, immediately south of downtown. But as Berlin started to revitalize there was the development of new events that needed the larger footprint available on Main Street. This is a trend that continues to this day.

For large parades and events during the Christmas holidays, the Town of Berlin police receive and give support to the neighboring towns of Ocean City, Snow Hill, and Pocomoke. Chief Downing also noted all the local police agencies participate in providing security for the annual Worcester County Fair. The primary focus for the police is to provide general safety at the parades. "We make sure the sidewalk is safe for the greater number of pedestrians and to make sure they do not accidentally get on the roadway where they may be endangered by vehicles." Downing also said the Berlin Police Department has a long and mutually supportive relationship with the Berlin Volunteer Fire Department and Emergency Medical Services.

The Berlin Police Department also works closely with the local Chamber of Commerce or Berlin Arts Council. "We begin preplanning with the sponsors weeks before an event and we always do a walk-through with them so we can address details, even small things or unique concerns," Chief Downing said. The shortest special events are five hours long during the day and the longest can last all weekend, from Friday evening through Sunday afternoon. Police responsibilities include working with the state and county to create motor vehicle detours, erecting electronic signs to direct motorists, and blocking the downtown Main Street area from motorists. In addition to No Thru Traffic signs and barriers, this also includes specially marked barrels to help guide motorists away from closed streets and toward the alternative routes. Message boards direct motorists to offsite parking.

Another service the police department provides is working with the town to put up temporary No Parking signs with the date and times of the restriction a few days before the event. These are highly visible and include any staging areas. The enforcement does not start until the morning before the event, but Berlin police also visit the downtown second story apartment residents prior to all special events to inform them of the posting of the temporary no parking zones. This allows these downtown residents to relocate their vehicles and avoid being ticketed or towed. Chief Downing also noted that as a result of the planning and coordination between the sponsors, town services, and the police department, most of the cleanup is completed within an hour or less after an event has ended. "With the support of town public works employees and volunteers, the streets are swept, trash cans emptied, all traffic signs and barriers are removed, and very quickly downtown shows no evidence that the event ever happened," he said.

A Halloween Mecca

A holiday tradition that has become a major attraction regionally for Berlin is the annual Halloween trick-or-treat celebration. Over the years nearby communities have either banned or discouraged Halloween activities, but Berlin has become a regional mecca for this traditional October celebration. This event is held for two to three hours in the early evening each Halloween. The attraction of so many costumed locals and guests has created a seemingly spontaneous event that dissipates as quickly as it begins. Downing noted that part of Main Street is closed to motor vehicles during Halloween and is transformed into a procession of trick or treaters. This is all done without disruption and even attracts appreciative adults who watch all the colorful downtown activities.

Some neighborhoods in town also request their streets be blocked from all motor vehicle traffic during the Halloween celebration. Residents elaborately decorate the exteriors of their homes and are dressed in costumes as they greet trick or treaters. But like all other town events, residents and volunteers work together. And happily, about an hour after the celebration ends there is almost no evidence that it ever happened.

Changes for Connectivity

Ivy Wells noted that "Berlin still needs more sidewalks to provide connectivity for downtown pedestrians, and our town needs to put in a bike trail that will connect downtown to Berlin's Heron Park." Wells said her department is applying for a state grant that would help to make the bike trail possible. She added that while visitors want to be a part of Berlin's small-town charm, residents also enjoy the added benefit of being able to ride a bike or walk to work as part of their daily routines.

Baked Dessert owner Robin Tomaselli said she anticipates more subtle changes will be coming to downtown. "I am looking forward to the day in the not-too-distant future when the Town of Berlin will no longer allow parking at any time along downtown Main Street," Tomaselli said. "We have so many pedestrians and shoppers that they will just step out between parked vehicles to visit another downtown location. Because of our charming old town feeling they tend to forget they must still deal with traffic." Ernie Gerardi, Berlin resident and owner of several town properties added, "As Berlin grows in popularity one of the key issues that it must focus on to maintain its vitality is that it must provide sufficient downtown parking. Without enough parking it will hurt the downtown businesses."

During my years as mayor, the suggestion was made to redevelop an area downtown into a public parking garage. However, this idea was not received favorably by most residents from either an aesthetic or safety standpoint. An alternative I believe should be explored is the creation of open-air parking on a second level above Berlin's largest parking lot. Purchase of the property could be financed along with design and construction costs. It should be well-landscaped, include the town's historic streetlamps, and be built with exteriors that complement, not diminish, our downtown's historic charm.

Another alternative is to provide trolley or tram services from Berlin's Heron Park on Old Ocean City Boulevard to and from downtown. The existing railroad tracks between Heron Park and downtown would make tram service a potential reality. Trolleys traveling by road, or a tram operating on the railroad track in town, could be maximized during special events and holidays. They also could provide convenient access to downtown on a daily basis on a smaller scale throughout the year.

CHAPTER ELEVEN

Destination Marketing in the Digital Age

J ust because your town is working to become a successful destination community, it is not necessarily top-of-mind for your potential guests. Fortunately, reaching out to new-comers has never been more cost-effective than it is now. Through websites, targeted messaging, and digital technology, you have the ability to quickly reach prospective guests at relatively lower costs than ever before.

By using a combination of digital and traditional communications you can bring attention and appeal to your community quickly and at low cost. In the early years of Berlin's revitalization there had been little coordinated effort to publicize or advertise the town. But as revitalization developed and the historic streetscape became an attraction, it was obvious the downtown would benefit from greater promotion.

Get to Know Your Partners

When our first economic development director, Michael Day, retired, he was succeeded in 2014 by Ivy Wells. Wells continues to take tourism in revitalized Berlin to a new level. Since beginning her tenure, the town has received twenty-eight of its thirty regional and national awards and certifications. Wells said from her experience the key elements to attracting visitors to a town are to know your audience, expand your resources, and don't focus on just one way of reaching out. "It's important to ensure good relationships with the press while also using a variety of social media." Wells added, "You must get to know your partners. You cannot operate like an island. You constantly reach out to others to learn from them and share your story."

"I stay connected to other economic development directors throughout the country by attending conferences, keeping up with news and trends, and always sharing and learning," Wells said. Berlin also works closely with tourism partners at the state and county levels to learn where guests are coming from. "We have a questionnaire at the town Welcome Center and at our Ambassadors Stand," Wells explained. "For example, in Berlin we have a lot of people who come from Pennsylvania, so we expand our advertising to reach well beyond our boundaries. Even though we are located just south of Delaware, our county tourism office even puts billboards as far north as highways in Pennsylvania."

Wells said Berlin attempts to appeal to all ages of people from all backgrounds. "What is appealing to the older generation is different from what appeals to the younger generation." She also noted that while having a strong social media presence is very important, print is not dead. The town invests in brochures, maps, guides, and print ads. "People like to have something tangible to hold, to save and to put on their refrigerator at home and look at," Wells said. Berlin's revitalization has always centered on restoring its historic look and downtown streetscape. So, it was natural when Berlin won acclaim as *America's Coolest Small Town* in 2014 that the town's economic development office reached out to *Preservation* magazine. An article on the history and architecture of the Hotel Atlantic was a big hit and Berlin continues to work with the publication to promote Berlin, Wells explained.

Succeeding in Social Media

The town's social media presence has also increased its visibility with posts on the international website platform Tripadvisor. Berlin worked to be included in a list of historic towns in the U.S. It also included a section where guests post online comments about their experience when they visit. "The presence on Tripadvisor continues to make a big difference in our exposure," Wells said. "We also have a weekly newsletter that asks our visitors to rate us and post pictures from their time in Berlin, including posts on Tripadvisor. People see what others are saying about our town and are enticed to visit us."

Wells noted that Berlin has embedded hot links in the town's online photos that automatically take web visitors to Downtown Berlin's website: www.berlinmainstreet.com. It includes a downtown map and parking, places to eat and drink, events, shopping, and local art. It also includes a downtown audio tour. Berlin's economic development director also has significantly increased its presence on Facebook. Starting with only 1,700 followers, the Town of Berlin now has over 20,000 followers and that number continues to grow. "We worked to make our Facebook page more engaging by posting many more photos, including town events, social media contacts, and special online contests. Winners of the online contests also receive a free gift from one of our downtown merchants."

Another effective digital format has been the development of more Instagram followers. "We started with 200 but now have more than 5,000 followers. Posting photos of people in Berlin enjoying life in our town has been another key to success. If we have a snowfall, we post a photo of a snowman and kids," Wells said. "Throughout the year people love seeing community members having a good time in our town. Others will see the post and say we need to go there. That looks like a good time. They will follow our posts and visit when they can." Wells explained digital marketing also reaches multiple generations and people of all racial and ethnic backgrounds. "We reach out to a variety of audiences. We make sure everyone is welcome and that we are an inclusive community, including broad support for ADA (Americans with Disabilities) and that we are pet friendly."

Wells noted that with revitalization, the community realized it needed to attract and appeal to visitors to support our downtown businesses and became part of the National Main Street Network. "We worked on improving our search engine optimization for Google and added many more key words that include historic tours, visit downtown, and events all aimed at targeting our marketing," Wells added. "We realized the most important thing about our town marketing is that we have become an 'eyes down' society because people are always looking at their phones. If you are not in someone's phone you aren't anywhere." To accomplish a high online and mobile presence we must update our town website and keep up all changes, especially about upcoming activities or events.

"On our town website we emphasize what will be happening for the next three months and the next three big things," Wells added.

Branding Your Community

Every product and every place should have a brand. "Berlin's branding is not just its historic setting but a place you can go and feel like a kid again," Wells emphasized. "No matter your age, you can come here and feel comfortable riding bicycles, joining sing-alongs, or even dancing in the street at our events without being judged. People can relax and take photos with funny poses, wear casual clothes or funny outfits and know if they come to Berlin, they will fit in." Important to Berlin's continued revitalization is that everyone feels welcome. Wells added, "When you come here you will find people just like you. Emotions are everything and it's important that when visitors come, they have a positive experience." Wells explained, "Berlin is part of the Beach to Bay Heritage Area and each community cross-promotes each other through that nonprofit group. Once a month, tourism representatives from each of the towns in our county meet to discuss ways we can promote each other." Wells also said another benefit is that this group also coordinates events to minimize dates of conflict for local events held in the five communities in Worcester County.

Lisa Challenger, who served as Worcester County's tourism director from 1989 until 2020, is known for being exceptionally creative and taking a positive approach to new challenges or opportunities. Challenger was a founding member of the Lower Eastern Shore Heritage Council and spearheaded numerous projects and programs that contributed to the growth of tourism in Berlin and Worcester County. Challenger is currently the director for the Lower Eastern Shore of Maryland's Beach to Bay Heritage Area.

"The obvious reason tourism is good for small towns is that people are attracted to vibrant places with merchants and restaurants that always emphasize quality," she said. Challenger also noted an old adage: Tourists bring money, then they go home. "It is always great to see stores and sidewalks filled with people carrying shopping bags. The attitude of looking upon others as strangers has never gotten anybody anywhere. People are willing to travel to have enjoyable, good experiences.

"Successful destinations always have people working as partners and sharing the work to become good hosts to visitors. In Berlin it took local people to invest in themselves and their businesses first. They did not look for financial help from the state or other government programs," Challenger added. "Communities have the opportunity to complement their activities and experiences by offering something different from other towns. Often visitors use one town as their base and then visit other nearby towns to expand and vary their experiences. It has long been known that many people come to Berlin to avoid the crowds at the beach in Ocean City. Then they visit other nearby towns to enjoy hiking, nature trails, kayaking, canoeing, and other outdoor activities. They will visit local museums and other historic places of interests."

Two programs that have greatly benefited Berlin and work with each other all over Maryland are the Main Street

Program and the Arts & Entertainment District. By obtaining those designations, a town creates not only good visitors but becomes eligible for state grants to promote tourism. "We cross-promoted both programs and created a brochure that showed multiple towns and their varied attractions," Challenger said. "They were not exclusive to one town and even the State of Delaware tourism department joined with us in a similar promotion. This allowed us to promote tourism throughout all of Delaware and Maryland's Eastern Shore. By coordinating and sharing we all get good ideas about what works and why."

Another local tourism professional is Melanie Pursel.

Melanie Pursel

After directing Ocean City, Maryland tourism for thirteen years, she is now serving as the tourism director for Worcester County. Pursel notes that Berlin was the first small town in our area to cultivate tourists, but this has approach has spread more recently throughout Worcester County. Pursel said, "Tourists in an area can be shared, they are not consumed and disappear after visiting just one town. Something that works in one town may not in another, because each town has its own appeal and experiences. And it is the same for a county or region."

Growing by Sharing

Ocean City has been a major tourist attraction on the beach for over a century and for much of that time it was seashore-centric. But Pursel said that recently there has been a successful outreach of sales directors and hospitality groups in the beach resort to collaborate and share with partners in nearby towns. "This collaboration with new partners is showing real signs of success. It keeps tourists in the area for longer stays."

In the most recent collaboration, merchants, Chambers of Commerce, local residents, and local government representatives meet five times a year for what they call Maryland Coast Mixers. Pursel said each of Worcester County's five communities host one of the mixers in a social setting. The effort is based on keeping tourists who visit the resort occupied within the area rather than traveling to another destination. "Ideas are freely exchanged on what can bring more tourists to each community and there is a spontaneous sharing of pride. People take ownership of the potential for tourism growth in each area and cooperate and share to support each other," she added. Pursel also noted that towns need to be business-friendly if they want to experience successful revitalization. In the county seat of Snow Hill, the town government is embracing mixed uses for older buildings. "They have found a need for their long-time zoning to be more flexible and practical." She added that another town, Pocomoke City, recently approved the establishment of a brewery where the code had never anticipated this use. You have to take risks to get a reward, but it also has a snowball effect. "There are always risks, but local government can make it easier for businesses to open. Communities must find ways to say 'yes', instead of instinctively saying 'no'," she said.

"This will spark tourism and the revitalization of downtowns we have seen in Salisbury and Berlin and are hoping to see in Snow Hill and Pocomoke." Pursel notes these include, "the restoration and repurposing of historic buildings into brew pubs, upgrading living spaces to create higher-end apartments, and converting old buildings to appealing retail spaces or restaurants." She also recommends making communities walkable, beautiful, and providing convenient signage for wayfinding.

But from the beginning and throughout ongoing revitalization, Pursel says, "It is a key part of your town's growth to determine what businesses make sense and fit within your identity. This process requires that guidelines are in place to ensure that you maintain the integrity of your community." There is also an ongoing need to keep a record of where visitors are coming from and who they are. "This helps you to identify new markets for visitors and go for them."

Pursel notes that it is not only okay, but an advantage, to have more than one restaurant, hair salon, bank, florist, bakery, or coffee shop and other visitor-friendly businesses in a downtown. She added, "This diversity attracts more people to a town and through collaboration will build a sense of pride and excitement about your community among business owners and residents."

Pursel added that all communities must find a balance between embracing tourism and enjoyable small-town living. A balance is always possible. "Visitor spending creates more revenues for small businesses but also improves or adds more amenities to a town." Pursel added, "Our experience is that the success of one community can lead to success in a neighboring community, but each finds a way within its unique personality. In this way they don't compete but instead complement each other." The appeal and experiences of each community provide more reasons for visitors to stay longer in an area or to come back at other times of the year. By communicating and coordinating between communities each town finds its own personality and this provides more points of interest for visitors to stay or return to the area.

CHAPTER TWELVE

It's Never Too Late
to Turn Your Town Around

"It's never too late to revitalize your community," Lisa Challenger said. "Older towns have historic structures and layouts. They are the bones of any town and they can be brought back to life. Many visitors are looking to get back to that small town experience. Every town has stories, history, and charm. This is true even if that town has become rundown." Challenger said communities should not expect or wait for outsiders to begin their revitalization. "It all goes hand-in-hand. Locals must have a stake in it. The revitalizing of businesses and older homes creates the setting for a great market. This will not only attract tourists, but also more people will move into what once may have been seen as a dying town." She added, "They must have a reason to visit and creating a thriving Main Street downtown is a great place to start."

Ivy Wells explained, "It's never, ever too late to turn your town around. The key is building relationships with downtown property owners. Without that your town's revitalization will have limitations. *Believing* is important but absolutely *wanting it*, is important just as much," Wells said. Berlin bed and breakfast innkeeper Jan Quick added, "I agree that it's never too late, but every town must find their niche. None of us like change but for things to be better you have to make changes that will make your town more welcoming. In our town we have encouraged the return of a more historic look through the restoration of our buildings. Years ago, when Berlin experienced the modernization of downtown, many people started to realize that this had been the wrong direction for our town." Fortunately, almost no historic downtown buildings in Berlin were torn down, but an identical twin residence that was next door to the Taylor House Museum had been purposely demolished and continues to be one of Berlin's greatest losses during the town's temporary movement toward modernization in the 1960s and '70s.

Jan Quick's husband, Jim, grew up in Toms River, New Jersey and had experienced firsthand the postwar economic transformation by tourism of his hometown. Years later, in 1986, Jim and Jan Quick were in their 30s and living near Berlin. The Quicks had just returned from a skiing trip when they were driving in Berlin and went past the old Holland House. They noticed a For Sale sign on the Bay Street property. The home had been built between 1910 and 1915. Starting with Dr. Charles Holland, the home had served as the residence and medical offices for four generations of doctors. It had also temporarily served as a maternity hospital during the late depression years and most of World War II. Jan said, "We were encouraged to buy the former Holland House property on Bay Street by Berlin local historian and attorney, Ed Hammond." The Hotel Atlantic was still undergoing extensive renovation and Hammond was one of the investors in that major renovation project.

The Quicks were also provided with encouragement by Renaissance Plaza developer and downtown businessman Bill Freeman. The couple, believing Berlin had all the elements to be a great small town by attracting visitors, made the purchase and immediately started converting the residence into a bed and breakfast. Jim and Jan hired the same contractor, Larry Widgeon, who was renovating the historic hotel. "Our B&B and the Hotel Atlantic worked well from the very start. We did not see ourselves as competitors, but both believed Berlin had great potential for guests," Jan said. "In the summer months you had 350,000 people driving by Berlin but didn't know about our town or what it was like. Instead, today and for many years we have had 1,000 or more people in Berlin on weekends." The Quicks bought the Holland House and have never looked back. Jan added, "Your perspective changes over time, but we are thankful we have been in the hospitality business as operators of the Holland House in Berlin for 37 years. Now all these years later, after putting in a lot of work and time every day, we know that initial feeling about the town's potential was right."

Jan continues to be impressed with the popularity of Berlin with guests. "Sometimes it feels like metro people come to our town in droves. I'm still amazed by how busy Berlin has become, especially on Saturdays and Sundays." She added, "The long-term effect has been that since the pandemic first hit, more people than ever want to be in smaller places and towns."

The Envy of Small Towns

Most of us have been conditioned into believing everything has an expiration date. This makes sense when the product or service is only temporarily available or has a finite shelf life. But when it comes to the potential to revitalize your town into a destination community, there is no date of expiration. It matters not how long since your town or region was in its heyday, the time when it achieved its greatest success, popularity, historical impact, or legacy. "Where there's a will there's a way." If someone is determined to do something, they will find a way to accomplish it regardless of obstacles. This is no different for communities than it is for individuals or families. In fact, a common denominator for revitalized towns is they are transformed by people who look at their communities as an extended family. "It's never too late to revitalize a town, but you not only have to do it right, but market it right," Treasure Chest owner Terri Sexton said. "I am very happy to see so many young families moving to Berlin and choosing this town as their home." She added, "Hopefully, their generation will continue to take Berlin's revitalization forward."

Another longtime believer in the town's revitalization, Berlin Police Chief Arnold Downing, agrees that it is never too late to begin making a town into a more welcoming place. Chief Downing noted, "These early downtown renovations began to make Berlin more inviting. All the downtown owners were local, and they started the transformation of the town into a more inviting place." The chief also noted that two of the largest businesses at that time were both operated by out-of-area chains, a Main Street supermarket and a discount retail store. "You can't wait or want outsiders to begin a town's restoration." Chief Downing added, "This process needs lots of interpersonal and face-to-face communications. But after the Berlin properties began a return to an earlier historic look, more businesses opened in downtown." Before the revitalization, the police chief noted that by 5 o'clock in the afternoon it appeared that most of downtown Main Street had "been rolled-up." This was at a time when most properties on the street were used for professional or business offices. And some downtown store locations had been converted to storage, but now they are now attractive, inviting retail businesses, and restaurants.

"But today," Downing added, "with so many places to shop and the opening of new restaurants, along with dessert and ice cream shops, our town now attracts people to stay not just during the day, but into the early evening." The chief also noted that since the beginning of downtown's historic restoration in the late 1970s many attractive stores and restaurants have opened. "The restoration of the Renaissance Plaza began to bring so many specialty shops to town. It is this variety of stores and nicer apartments that are the key to making Berlin unique."

The chief also said the establishment of a historic district by the Town of Berlin had accelerated the transition of downtown. "There is nothing gawdy or out of step in the appearance of historic Berlin. People from our town, not outsiders, made this happen," he added. Chief Downing is optimistic about the town's future because Berlin has discovered and continues to support historic revitalization. And Downing is very pleased that such improvements continue. One example he noted are the three contiguous historic buildings in the heart of downtown, owned by local developer Jack Burbage, that are now being restored to their earlier 19th century look. "We have a lot of history here and it started with the reconstruction of the Hotel Atlantic in 1895," after the first of Berlin's three big downtown fires. "Today we still have that 1895 feel when people come to visit and that feel is consistent," Chief Downing said.

"Berlin is the envy of small towns in America," said Hotel Atlantic operator John Fager. "When you invest it, you believe it and are compassionate about it, and it shows up in the result. Some of Berlin's key attractions are its southern hospitality where we welcome everyone like they are a friend and we are authentic, not an act or something that is rehearsed. This is who we are, and this is how we treat people. There is a sense of community here, a feeling of oneness that has developed over the last twenty to thirty years." This developed over time into mutual support—"what is good for one, is good for all."

Learning to Thrive on Change

The real estate market in less urban areas and smaller communities is experiencing historic sales rates. As the property values and prices of homes go up in less populated towns and regions, the potential number of home buyers is actually increasing, not diminishing. Existing families and retirees in urban and suburban areas are buying homes and moving to smaller communities for a variety of reasons. Families are now joining retirees as they seek places to live that are more safe, less frenetic, and where they can live and enjoy life in less congested communities. There is the added benefit of reduced stress from commuting to and from work compared to what residents are accustomed to in urban and suburban neighborhoods.

A longstanding trend in our small-town experience is a yearning by visitors to experience traditional American values. Often this is an overlooked asset of towns that have the potential to be a great place to live as well as visit.

Baked Dessert's Robin Tomaselli said from her experience over the past decade, she believes one person can make a big difference. "So, a larger group of people can make an even bigger difference in a relatively short time," she added. "In addition to being a small business owner, you can make a difference by also caring about the entire town. By attracting and welcoming visitors to our community you help the area to be healthy both culturally and fiscally. It's never too late to turn your town around. Particularly since the Covid pandemic, people all over the country are seeking to both visit and live in smaller more remote locations. That can certainly be seen in Berlin in the real estate market. As soon as a house is on the market, it is sold. Not because of pricing, but as a result of a greater influx of people from New York, New Jersey, and Pennsylvania."

She added, "This has been a longer-term trend but now is unprecedented as a result of the pandemic." Tomaselli said the continuing growth of visitors and residents are outcomes from more people being interested in experiencing small town living. "This has made our town more economically thriving. And shops busy with customers also mean higher employment for our residents. Even relatively new residents from nearby Delaware have an important impact on our community."

Another great example of this impact is Dreamweaver owner Tiffany Lackner, who said her downtown Berlin store continues to exceed her expectations. She believes the foundation of success is "Staying positive, staying firm in your faith, and not letting anything get in the way. If you do this and put your full effort into your business, then you can expect it to succeed." Lackner added, "You always have to consistently believe in what you are doing. Keep trying new things and when they work that's great, but if not, just move on. It's always important to do all you can to create love and strive to do better for your family and community."

Resident Ernie Gerardi also emphasized that for Berlin to continue to be a successful community it must always create a reason for young families to move into town. Gerardi added, "They are the ones who will create the leadership for our town in the future. And real leadership is about making your town welcoming and viable not just for now, but for future generations."

CHAPTER THIRTEEN

Your Town's Revitalization
Can Be Never Ending

Throughout this book, the revitalization of downtown Berlin, Maryland has been viewed from many perspectives. It is essential that this is understood as ongoing and not limited in time. The foundation of this ongoing process is a community's successful adaptation to changing times. The revitalization of Berlin is a great example of reinvigorating a community with new life and vitality while preserving its roots and history. This understanding should be a legacy that is handed down, transformed, and adapted from one generation to the next.

The stories that follow in this chapter illustrate that the lasting revitalization of a community can be ongoing and never-ending. As times change, so can adaptation and approaches. Each interview subject approached their work with varied backgrounds and perspectives, but all acted on a shared belief. While preserving the best of Berlin's heritage, each of them saw the opportunity to make a positive impact through their own distinctive contribution, one that would complement the legacy of all who came before.

This Could Be Something

This story begins when Caitlin LaComb and her husband Mike were living in Fredericksburg, Virginia. Caitlin and Mike both served in the U.S. Army, including tours overseas in East Africa. After their active service they became members of the U.S. Army Reserve. Their first child was born in February 2017 and a couple of years later they gave birth to a second child. The family continued to live in Fredericksburg for another three years.

During that time Caitlin experimented with numerous recipes for Key Lime pie and after about twenty versions she created a pie she felt had hit the mark and named it "The Floridian." Her husband suggested she make several more identical pies and sell them. Not long afterward, she began selling her special Key Lime pies at a Farmers Market about 45 minutes away from their home in Fredericksburg.

Caitlin LaComb

Caitlin received strong support and encouragement regarding making and selling pies from her husband Mike, who said, "This could be something." She began making many pies at home while learning about operating a business at the same time. Caitlin and Mike decided they needed a site to develop and grow the pie business, but retail rental costs anywhere near the vicinity of Washington, D.C. were simply too high.

It was at this time in 2019 that Caitlin's dad, Bill Cecil, a resident of Salisbury, Maryland, saw an ad on Facebook advertising a building for rent in Vienna, Maryland. The couple immediately visited the site on Maryland's Eastern Shore owned by the Town of Vienna. The building and the community had been on US 50 (Ocean Gateway) that for decades had been the major north-south route for motorists traveling from mid-Atlantic metro areas to Ocean City, Maryland. But in the 1980s the state of Maryland constructed a new bridge over the Nanticoke River and all major vehicle traffic bypassed Vienna.

Caitlin and Mike visited the rental location in Vienna and decided to start their pie shop there. Unfortunately, this was also the time the Covid pandemic was starting in America. Shortly after opening, the pie shop temporarily closed to retail customers due to the pandemic, but the LaCombs continued to make and sell pies on Saturdays at the farmer's market in Fredericksburg, Virginia.

The couple soon were able to reopen their pie shop in Vienna and shortly after they began selling their pies at the Berlin Farmers Market in 2021. The pies were an instant success, and they loved the potential they saw for business in downtown Berlin. They contacted Berlin's economic development director, Ivy Wells, but no locations in downtown were available for rent at that time. But in April 2022, Wells contacted the LaCombs again to inform them that a storefront had just become available for rent. It was located in downtown on William Street, across from Town Hall, and would be an ideal spot for their pie shop.

Caitlin and Mike visited the downtown Berlin location and immediately proceeded to rent the commercial space and begin renovations needed to transform the site into a pie shop. The new 'Mandala Pies' (pronounced Man-DAH-La) opened in Berlin in September 2022. The word *Mandala* has its origin in South Asia and is literally the geometric term for circle. It is also known for beautiful designs made with good intentions but that focus on the moment. Catlin said, "At Mandala Pies we concentrate on the process and the experience. Then with the eating enjoyment of our customers, it is wiped away."

The LaCombs now live in Salisbury, but it is their dream to own a home in the Berlin area. "We have always loved the beach and this area and feel all this is meant to happen," Caitlin said. "We really feel very welcomed here. This is a place that really appreciates friendship and community." The feeling for their move to the Eastern Shore of Maryland is reflected in their business slogan, "we bake beautiful pies for beautiful people."

Keeping it Fresh and Evolving

Cassandra and Randy Brown own and operate Una Bella Salute on South Main Street. Cassandra's grandfather, Riley Robins, who was born in the early 1900s, had the family's first business in downtown Berlin when he operated a barbershop in the 1950s. Cassandra has extended and expanded the family legacy with the Una Bella Salute. "Randy and I always wanted to operate a business, but never expected to have a shop in downtown Berlin." Their store sells a large variety of fresh extra virgin olive oils from around the world and along with balsamic vinegar from Modena, Italy. These olive oils are used for cooking, marinades, dressings and many other recipes. They also sell fresh pastas and many gourmet products.

Una Bella Salute first opened on Broad Street in 2014 and

was bought by Cassandra and Randy in 2018. They nurtured the business, and it soon outgrew the original space so they moved their shop to its larger current location at 6 South Main Street. Cassandra and Randy have greatly expanded the customer base for their shop and now have many customers from Pennsylvania, New York, Washington, D.C., the western shore of Maryland and also some

Cassandra Brown

from New Jersey. In keeping with Berlin's transition to a destination community, "We now have more customers who are visitors to our town, then we do who are locals," Cassandra said. "A great number of our clientele are repeat customers who come back often, especially if it is a cloudy or rainy day at the beach."

Many of their visiting customers become regulars who shop Una Bella Salute any time they are in the Berlin area. "Once they have visited our town, on later trips they bring groups of friends and relatives," she explained. "About 25 percent of our customers are locals, another 25 percent are new to our store, and 50 percent are repeat customers from all over.

They like the uniqueness of our shop and of our town and appreciate that the downtown stores do not carry the same goods." Cassandra said they also mail their products both near and far. We get orders online and then we mail them to places as far away as California, Seattle, Washington, or upstate New York.

The Browns have a lot of experience and success with social media. They also believe that Berlin's exposure on the town's website, especially the events page, has greatly benefited not only their business but many others throughout downtown. "Special events and festivals attract people to the uniqueness of our town," Cassandra noted. As events have continued to evolve, they benefit more downtown shops. One example was the relatively recent decision to turn the southernmost stage for town events to a parallel position on Main Street. This simple move has not only enhanced downtown events but allows easy access to all the businesses along Berlin's South Main Street.

Cassandra is another strong believer in Berlin. She serves on the town's board of directors for the Chamber of Commerce and is actively involved in the successful efforts to refocus and revamp Berlin's Arts & Entertainment District. She stated, "We all should always strive to keep it fresh and keep evolving."

Creating a 'Commons' Culture

Brett Hines and his wife, Megan, started their professional lives as teachers in Colorado. While teaching, Brett also worked at a start-up business called Branch Out Cider. The firm sourced local apples and used the fruit's sugars for fermentation to produce alcohol. This process was accomplished on a small human scale and did not require a large distilling operation. Brett had always been someone who has worked with his head and been a strong advocate for environmental health. The idea of making an alcoholic beverage from

Brett Hines

fruit was very appealing to him. This was the beginning of an idea that Brett would refine and develop when he and Megan returned to Worcester County in 2014. A year later the couple moved to a home they purchased in Berlin. After moving back to Maryland's Eastern Shore, they began networking with local farmers to develop sources for the fruits they would need to develop their own business, now known as the Buzz Meadery.

The meadery takes local fruits and makes honey that ultimately is made into a drink that can be 4 to 8 percent alcohol by volume, and then is carbonated. The result is called session mead and requires that people who drink it be at least 21 years of age. The Hines' first started selling the mead drink at local farmers markets on the Lower Eastern Shore. "We did all of this on high school teachers' salaries," Brett said. "And we want people to know that if you have a vision, back it up with a plan and work. It can be done." He added, "We not only want to be a part of the business community, but also part of the local culture."

They introduced their new mead product at Berlin's Farmers Market, which they continue to do. But they also wanted to provide a downtown public area where people could picnic and experience the local culture. The Hines's created a green grass area in 2021, at the intersection of Jefferson and Gay Streets, and added traditional wood fencing and picnic tables behind the Hotel Atlantic. They named this public space the *Berlin Commons*. During the year special events are held at the Commons where local craftsman sell art crafts and products. The Commons also is the site of some activities when the Town of Berlin is hosting special events throughout the year.

Their vision did not end with the Berlin Commons and in 2022 they opened the Jun & Juice shop on Pitts Street in the heart of downtown Berlin. All the fresh beverages they sell are made from local ingredients. "Our clientele is about evenly split 50-50 between locals and visitors," Brett said. "And we have found a lot of people come from across the Chesapeake Bay, or areas to the north, and really do come back." Through their hard work and efforts to establish their business model in Berlin, the Hines's seek to lead by example rather than being limited to a role of informing, as they were as teachers.

Reinventing Jewelry as Art

Michele Krempa spent her youth in Baltimore and earned her college degree from Loyola University. After leaving the state, she moved back to Maryland in 2011 and now lives in Delmar. Shortly after her move to the area, Krempa soon started a wholesale jewelry business in Salisbury. Her business quickly developed and she decided that she would like to complement the enterprise with the addition of retail sales. But she was not sure where the right location was on the

Lower Eastern Shore. Krempa had been a jewelry vendor for

twenty years at both the annual Springfest and Sunfest celebrations in Ocean City. She looked at locations along the coast including West Ocean City, but after a visit to that area decided it was not the right place for a

Michele Krempa

business to attract people who appreciate the creative work that she does. Krempa now has two businesses at her Berlin Main Street location, Beach Memories and Seaschelle Designs.

Krempa had always enjoyed shopping in downtown Berlin and met with downtown landlord Ernie Gerardi for an "interview" for one of his Main Street store locations. "After showing him my business plan we both agreed it was a perfect location for my businesses," Krempa said. "It was a win-win situation for both of us. It was not only a great place for a retail shop but would enable me to also continue my wholesale business that served all of the United States and the Caribbean." She opened the Berlin shop in August 2019.

"Here at our store, we take all kinds of beads and reinvent them. We are one of a very few American jewel makers who do this in the U.S. Our customers very much are attracted to the creativity of our jewelry," Krempa said. "We even make beads that are filled with remains from cremation. People bring in some of the cremated remains of a loved one and we fill and design beads for them." She explained that relocating her business in Berlin has been great for attracting tourists, but also locals who keep coming back. "The Main Street location attracts the perfect demographic for my products—women between the age of 35 to 70 who have some disposable income and who appreciate the art in our work," Krempa said. "All of our inventory is handmade and people watch what we are doing and usually buy something." While the wholesale business has grown, so have retail sales and the expanding locations of shoppers." She added. "A lot of people come from Pennsylvania and more and more from all over the country, even California. We even have shoppers occasionally from as far away as Japan and China."

As with all downtown businesses, retail sales are best between spring through New Year's. But in the winter months of January and February, with her 22 years of experience, Krempa provides classes to teach making beads. Krempa says the next step for her business is to start blowing glass and making bigger pieces of jewelry. Krempa notes that the number of arts employees is growing, and she now has two graduates of Salisbury University who earned bachelors' degrees in hot glass. Krempa said she is thankful for the support she receives from other downtown businesses and is also very happy with the successful efforts of Ivy Wells, the town's downtown development director, in attracting people and promoting Berlin. "Ivy does a phenomenal job," she added.

Berlin's Siren of the Sea

Alyssa Maloof's idea for the world's first Mermaid Museum in downtown Berlin all started with the space. Her dad was a professional photographer. When she was very young,

Alyssa Maloof

Alyssa accompanied her dad on a photo shoot on the second floor of Berlin's historic Odd Fellows Building, which is now the upstairs location of this unique and fun museum. Even at a young age she had been impressed with the Victorian aesthetic that filled every corner of the room including the large chandelier that hung from the center of the ceiling. Although Maloof grew up in the small town of Quantico, on Maryland's Lower Eastern Shore, as an adult she later moved to Philadelphia, Pennsylvania, and like her dad, became a professional photographer. She moved to Berlin in 2018. About three years later she learned the upstairs of the Odd Fellows building was available for lease and made an appointment to see it again. It was apparent that the Victorian Era aesthetic had been retained and matched the well-preserved look of the entire building. Maloof said she was attracted to the vintage feel of the place and immediately knew, "This was where I was meant to be."

Maloof worked intensely on the space for about six months and by March 2021 she was ready to open another aspiration that she had cultivated over time, a Mermaid Museum. "I had always been into mermaids and always had loved art," she said. "So, I prepared my mermaid-themed business to be a mix of history and fun stuff." Today her Mermaid Museum displays many mermaid-themed objects and artifacts.

She even has a rare, preserved mermaid that generations ago, famous 19th century American showman P.T. Barnum had at one time displayed.

The Mermaid Museum, located on Jefferson Street next to the Hotel Atlantic, features many artifacts and items of interest on display. The museum is anchored by a big fountain under the central ornate chandelier and features many displayed objects, a drawing wall, a giant seashell, a mermaid bathtub and a mermaid's tail. She also has places for visitors to draw, create photo opportunities and video presentations. She also provides multimedia pieces, peepholes and other multi-dimensional attractions that are enjoyed by both kids and adults. Maloof continues to make new additions and installations to the museum. She is very pleased that her unique place attracts many new people to town. Maloof said, "I know the Mermaid Museum gets a lot of people to come to Berlin and those visitors really enjoy going to our town's other downtown businesses."

Thriving In Changing Times

Susan Ayres Wimbrow has deep roots in Berlin. Her great-grandfather James and his brother John built the existing brick building at 7-9 South Main Street in 1901 after one of the town's great fires at the turn of the 20th century. The Ayres Brothers owned and operated a general store from the Main Street site while James's sisters, Amanda and Mary Anna, were the next-door proprietors of a millinery shop. The building in back, near the westernmost point on Bay Street, is now the site of Baked Dessert Café. When it was built by the

Ayres brothers, the building originally served as the office for their Main Street stores.

During the early years of the 20th century, downtown Berlin was thriving with businesses. In 1910 Berlin adopted

Susan Ayres Wimbrow

"Watch Berlin Grow!" as its slogan. The Ayres family stores were part of that growth. Later each of the sisters would own separate hotels in Ocean City. Amanda was born in Ocean City in 1877 and was possibly the first baby to be born in the early seaside village. She and her husband bought the Shoreham Hotel in the 1920s. The other sister, Mary Anna, and her husband, built the Lankford Hotel on the boardwalk in 1924.

Today, Susan Ayres Wimbrow continues the family tradition of creating new business ventures. Berlin did not have an independent bookstore prior to the opening of The Greyhound An Indie Bookstore in 2018. Susan and her husband Maury had rescued greyhounds for over 20 years. During that time, they have owned three greyhounds. Wimbrow said, "Greyhounds are an elegant dog and have an English feel." It was also at this time that she was considering writing a book from her experiences in her over forty-year career in the funeral home business. "I had always wanted to write a fiction book. It is entitled *Death Is My Life* and was an opportunity to share some very bizarre stories I had experienced as a funeral director." She started writing the book after receiving strong encouragement and support from Barbara Lockhart, a friend and the author of several adult and children's books, all celebrating the Eastern Shore. After publishing her first novel, Susan also did podcasts for the purpose of helping people to heal who have lost loved ones to murder.

Wimbrow added, "Our town has become a fine arts mecca. I believe books and fine arts complement each other. I believe Berlin is an enchanting, charming, hallmark of a town. All the merchants are so friendly. Many people who come to Berlin have been going to Ocean City for years. When they do visit, they ask themselves, Why haven't we come here before?"

Wimbrow attributes some of Berlin's popularity to the many family-oriented special events the community hosts each year. She also thinks it is very important for downtown merchants to offer diverse merchandise and not compete to provide the same things. "Every store is different. The common trait they have is the friendliness and the willingness to help visitors understand what's available in town," Wimbrow said. She added her thanks for everyone who shops local. "If you visit our small town you have to shop on Main Street and throughout our downtown. Berlin is a great example of a culture that wants to see small town America thrive."

Berlin has changed to meet different economic and social circumstances during its existence. As in the past, it continues to adapt and change, but with an understanding and awareness of how it must always be a welcoming place. It is for each new generation of residents, community leaders and businesses, to make the decisions and provide the example so this evolution of revitalization never ends.

It's Time—Wait No More!

Hopefully it comes as no surprise that what you believe has so much to do with what you get out of life. The same is true for your town. With the telling of the stories in this book, it is my hope that many individuals, groups and towns will be inspired to take a new look at their community—to recognize its history and untapped potential for enjoyment and success, not only now, but in the years and generations ahead.

An ancient proverb says, "A journey of a thousand miles begins with a single step." This old saying is particularly appropriate to the task of revitalizing your community. Do not let the totality of the effort overwhelm you or cause procrastination. With both belief and resolve you and fellow citizens can obtain big achievements that often begin with small, but concrete steps.

If you have been waiting for the right time to begin...wait no more!

EPILOGUE

From my own lifetime of experience in Berlin, growing up here, serving as a long-time newspaper editor, public servant, and former mayor, I have learned it is essential to believe in your town's potential. But just as importantly, you must have the desire to roll up your sleeves and go to work to make it blossom into a vibrant, successful destination community. As I have often said about Berlin, "Unlike many small towns, we are not intimidated by change—we thrive on it."

Ultimately, you too can nurture an understanding and appreciation for what your community can mean to both your residents and potential guests. This will enable you and other people in your town to know what to preserve and what to change—and knowing this makes all the difference. A promising future is made possible by those who prepare for it. Remember that the race to the bottom is a race to a bottomless pit. If you are always looking for the cheapest way to do something, not the best way, don't be surprised by disappointing results. It is essential that your town's elected and appointed leaders work with citizens and property owners if you wish to transform your downtown into a successful destination community.

When you welcome guests into your community the idea is not to have them just shop, eat, or visit, but to enjoy a delightful experience they will want to share with others. Life in a welcoming town is not meant to be suffered but celebrated. As you *turn your town around* look for a variety of opportunities to celebrate life while keeping in mind that many of your dreams cannot be fully accomplished by any one generation. But with a foundation of kindness, tolerance, and mutual respect between residents and visitors, your community can build a bridge to the future that is founded not only on the past but is complemented with inviting and tasteful innovations. Ultimately, as you transform your community into an enjoyable destination and the more you honor your town's past, the more opportunity you will have in the future.

One thing that sets Berlin apart is our quality of life. Both residents and guests share a genuine sense of community. And as time passes people who live and visit here feel they are part of a larger family. Our town consistently leads the way regionally in developing a culture of tolerance and respect for all people—regardless of their race, religion, or place of origin. Although our beautiful late Victorian Era architecture makes a great first impression, our classic American values demonstrate daily that the way we live, work, and share our community is what truly makes Berlin a special place. I sincerely believe that first-time visitors, or folks who have not been to our town in many years, will find the experience to be an unexpected pleasure.

It is with this in mind that I share with you a timeless quote from Ralph Waldo Emerson, a man of letters known for championing self-reliance, that I believe is particularly appropriate for our community's history and can be for yours.

"Do not go where the path may lead. Go instead where there is not a path and leave a trail."

ACKNOWLEDGMENTS

JEFF AUXER—Founder and owner-operator of Jeffrey Auxer Designs.

PATTY BACKER—Founder and owner-operator of the Dusty Lamb.

JAY BERGEY, CPA — Founder and owner-operator of Bergey & Company, PA, Certified Public Accountants.

CASSANDRA BROWN—Co-owner and operator of Una Bella Salute.

LISA CHALLENGER —Formerly, Worcester County tourism director for 31 years; currently. director of the Lower Eastern Shore of Maryland's Beach to Bay Heritage Area.

DONNA COMPHER—Founder and owner-operator of Sisters Gift & Wine Bar.

MICHAEL DAY—Former economic development director of Berlin (2005 - 2014).

ARNOLD DOWNING—Berlin chief of police and board member of Worcester Youth & Family Counseling.

DAVE ENGLEHART—Planning director for Town of Berlin.

JOHN FAGER—Operator of Berlin's historic Hotel Atlantic and also owner of Fager's Island and the Lighthouse Club hotel in Ocean City.

BILL FREEMAN—Early believer in revitalizing downtown Berlin and former owner of the Treasure Chest Jewelry Shop.

DEBBIE SMITH FRENE—Founder and former co-owner of Victorian Charm and early downtown believer.

STEVE FRENE—Former co-owner of Victorian Charm and active and longtime Berlin Chamber volunteer.

ERNIE GERARDI—Berlin resident who has remodeled and revitalized several town residential properties and three downtown Main Street commercial properties.

BRETT HINES—Founder and co-owner-operator of the Buzz Meadery, the Jun & Juice Shop and the Berlin Commons.

TIFFANY LACKNER—Founder and co-owner-operator of Dreamweaver.

CAITLIN LACOMB—Founder and co-owner-operator of Mandala Pies.

OLGA KOZHEVNIKOVA—Founder and owner-operator of the World of Toys.

MICHELLE KREMPA—Founder and owner-operator of Beach Memories and Seachelle Designs.

ALYSSA MALOOF—Founder and owner-operator of the Mermaid Museum.

JOE MOORE—Chair of the Berlin Planning & Zoning Appeals Board.

ANNA MULLIS—Director of the Worcester County Arts Council.

BILL OUTTEN—Berlin resident and owner-operator of three downtown antiques stores.

J.E. PARKER—Former Berlin council member and owner of downtown Main Street commercial property.

MELANIE PURSEL—Worcester County tourism director.

MIKE QUEEN—Berlin resident and owner-operator of Rayne's Reef Café and other Main Street commercial properties.

JAN QUICK—Co-owner-operator of Holland House Bed & Breakfast.

MELISSA REID—President of Berlin Heritage Foundation & Museum.

CAROL ROSE—Former chair and current member of Berlin Historic District Commission.

TERRI SEXTON—Treasure Chest owner-operator & former Berlin Chamber board member.

SUSAN TAYLOR—Curator of the Berlin Heritage Foundation & Calvin B. Taylor Museum.

ROBIN TOMASELLI—Co-owner-operator of Baked Dessert Café.

IVY WELLS—Town of Berlin's economic development director (2014 – present).

SUSAN AYRES WIMBROW—Co-owner-operator of The Greyhound An Indie Bookstore.

TOWN OF BERLIN
AWARDS & CERTIFICATIONS

- Most Charming Small Town in Maryland — Trips to Discover – 2022
- *Esquire*: Charming American Towns to Visit – 2022
- Berlin: One of the Best Places to Vacation - House Beautiful US, October 2021
- Tripadvisor Travelers Choice Award – 2021
- BuzzFeed: 18 Surprisingly Cool Small Towns In The USA: Berlin, MD – 2020
- The Best Small Town in Every State — Trip Savvy – 2020
- Traveler's Choice Award — Tripadvisor – 2020
- America's Best Small Town for Shopping — *USA Today* – 2020
- One of Most Charming Towns in America — *O, The Oprah Magazine* – 2020
- 12 of America's Up and Coming Small Towns — *Reader's Digest* – 2019
- National Small Business Saturday Innovation Champion: Main Street America – 2019
- 50 Most Beautiful Small Towns in the World — Love-Exploring.com – 2019

- Maryland's Most Beautiful Small Town — *House Beautiful* magazine – 2018
- America's Best Small Town for Shopping — *USA Today* – 2018
- Best Budget Destinations in America — *Budget Travel* magazine – 2018
- Electric Utility Reliability Award (Top 10% USA) — American Public Power – 2016
- Great American Main Street Award: (Top 10 USA)— National Main Street Center – 2016
- South's Best Small Towns — *Southern Living* magazine – 2016
- 20 Best Small Towns to Visit — Smithsonian.com – 2016
- 10 Most Enchanting, Magical Christmas Towns in Maryland — www.onlyinourstate.com – 2016
- 40 Charming American Towns You've Never Heard of But Should Visit ASAP — *House Beautiful* magazine – 2016
- Berlin Ambassadors Program — Governor's Service Award for Volunteerism – 2015
- 50 Most Beautiful Towns in America — *Good Housekeeping* magazine – 2015
- Heritage Tourism Event Award — Lower Eastern Shore Heritage Council – 2015
- Top Family Travel Spots on Maryland's Eastern Shore — *Budget Travel* magazine – 2015
- Top Things to do in *America's Coolest Small Town* — PBS Television – 2015

- Great Small Towns near DC — *Washingtonian* magazine – 2015
- Town Spirit Achievement Award — Maryland Municipal League – 2015
- Healthy Eating Active Living Town — Institute for Public Health Innovation – 2015
- Top 50 Most Beautiful Towns in America — *Country Living* magazine – 2015
- 10 Most Beautiful Towns in America — The Culture Trip – 2015
- Certificate of Excellence Award' — TripAdvisor – 2015
- Best Use of Social Media — Maryland Office of Tourism – 2014
- America's Coolest Small Town — *Budget Travel* magazine – 2014
- Maryland's Coolest Small Town — *The Baltimore Sun* – 2013
- Sustainable Maryland Certified Community (*First Town in Maryland*)
  University of Maryland Environmental Finance Center – 2012

www.berlinmainstreet.net

ABOUT THE AUTHOR

Gee Williams was born and raised in the Town of Berlin and his family has been involved in local and state politics since the 1940s. A graduate of the Stephen Decatur High School class of 1966, he and his wife Betsy have been married just over fifty years.

Gee was a member of the first graduating class of Chesapeake College in 1969. He then graduated with a bachelor's degree from the University of Maryland College Park in 1971, majoring in business and journalism. He served as a newspaper editor and publisher for thirty years, managing weekly publications along the East Coast from Delaware to South Carolina.

Since 2000, Gee worked in public relations, marketing and nature tourism for the Maryland Department of Resources and the Maryland State Highway Administration. He also served as marketing and development director for the Community Foundation of the Eastern Shore until his retirement in 2018.

Gee has devoted much time over the past forty-five years to civic and political service to improve the quality of life in his community. A life member of the Berlin Lions Club, he was first elected to the Berlin Town Council in 2003 and then served another twelve years as Berlin's Mayor until the fall of 2020.

He continues to be active in strengthening local environmental stewardship and revitalizing the Town of Berlin's economic vitality as a leader in Berlin's ongoing efforts to serve as an enjoyable destination community. Gee successfully lobbied the Maryland Legislature for two years (2010-2011) to win state approval to allow craft breweries to legally establish in Worcester County.

Since he first became active in public service for the Town of Berlin the community has grown from 3,000 to 4,500 residents. While serving as mayor, Berlin's Historic Downtown District became home to over seventy thriving small businesses, doubling the number that had previously existed. Also, during Gee's twelve years as mayor, the Town of Berlin received thirty unsolicited state and national awards and certifications, including *America's Coolest Small Town*.

A longtime member of the Maryland Mayors Association and the Maryland-Delaware-D.C. Press Association, Gee's current memberships include: the Local Leaders Council for Smart Growth America; the First and Main national coalition; the Maryland Academy for Climate Change; and Strong Towns, whose mission is to make communities of all sizes better today by creating places that are safe, livable and inviting.

Gee has received numerous newspaper and community service awards, including the 1988 Berlin Award, the 2021 R. Clayton Mitchell, Jr. Award for distinguished public service in Maryland, and the Sun Award for significant support to Worcester Youth and Family Services at their 45th annual celebration.

SPEAKING ENGAGEMENTS

The author of *Turn Your Town Around* provides professional speaking services and workshops that help towns, regardless of size, to overcome stagnation and chart a proven course towards becoming thriving destination communities.

CONTACT GEE WILLIAMS at:

turnyourtownaround.net

NAME INDEX*

---

*   *PI* designates mention in Photo Insert, following page 82.